C000085502

CHARLOTTE COR)
established artis
in fifteenth-century ᴉᴉᴛᴇʀᴀᴛᴜʀᴇ ᴏ... ᴘ......
three novels with Faber and Faber to critical
acclaim: *The Unforgiving* (1991), *The Laughter of
Fools* (1993) and *The Guest* (1996). She won an
Arts Council Award for her fiction. She has had
numerous original plays, short stories and drama
series commissioned by BBC Radio 4 and has
written regularly for the *Sunday Times*, *Daily
Telegraph*, *Country Life* and many others.

Cory's artworks, often described as 'visual short
stories', form an intriguing alternative 19th
century based on reworked, montaged Victorian
carte de visite photography. These have been
exhibited in galleries all over the world including
the Brontë Parsonage Museum in Haworth, the
Globe Theatre and the Sir John Soane's Museum
in London, and are in the Royal Collection
at Windsor. Charlotte Cory lives between
Greenwich, London, on the River Thames, and
Sancerre on the River Loire in central France.

The Lemon Painters is her first book of short stories
and marks her return to publishing fiction.

THE LEMON PAINTERS
SHORT STORIES

CHARLOTTE CORY

CALQUE PRESS

Text © Charlotte Cory 2020
Cover design © Vince Haig 2020
http://calquepress.com
ISBN: 978-1-9162321-2-9
Type: Hoefler Text

British Library Cataloguing-in-Publication Data
A catalogue record for this book is available from the
British Library

The right of Charlotte Cory to be identified as author
of this work has been asserted in accordance with
Section 77 of the Copyright, Designs and Patents Act
1988

Calque Press
An imprint of Nevsky Editions Ltd.
2020

CONTENTS

THE LEMON PAINTERS

THE SEQUENCE OF THINGS

MRS HOLT SMILES—EVER SO BRIGHTLY, STRAIGHT into my face—and she says: 'Now, Lucy, I want you to tell me *all* about when this photograph was taken'. And I am so surprised, I say, 'Oh, golly gosh, I beg your pardon!' and look around to see if I can escape, but there is no escape—we are at the end of a dark corridor and the patch of light nearby is not a doorway but a window set into the corridor with a window seat. Then I see she is holding out the very picture I have been doing my best to forget. The photograph of her son, Philip, taken the morning of his departure for France.

A photograph like tens of thousands of other photographs of fresh-faced young men in uniform, scattered across the mantelpieces of Europe like poppies in a cornfield.

I cannot believe this is happening. It is exactly what I have been doing my best to avoid, but before I can think, Mrs Holt has taken me by the arm and brought me into a small heavily furnished room with a fire burning in the grate. She shuts the door behind me, barring my escape, and I am trapped with her. Mummy and Daddy are downstairs with Mr Holt, and before she had shut the door I could hear the comforting buzz of their darling voices echoing in the far reaches of this cold rambling family home in the middle of nowhere. In the middle of Ireland. Goodness, we had a bother finding it the other day! But Mummy and Daddy might as well be back over the Irish Sea for all the help they can give me now. I am well and truly cornered. I think of all the moth-eaten foxes' heads mounted on wooden shields in the hallway downstairs and for a moment I have a vision of Mrs Holt wanting to add my own head to the gruesome collection.

But this is ridiculous. It was her idea that we should come here. 'It is what Philip would have liked,' she wrote to me. 'And we are so keen to meet you, Lucy.'

So I look at her hopelessly, hoping she might take pity and release me back into the long cold corridors of her house, but her grip on my arm tightens and she steers me over to a low embroidered chair by the fire. She pushes me down into the chair and thrusts the picture into my hands.

I have no choice but to take it, and for the first time in years, I look at—Philip! The picture is faded now, and not at all easy to see clearly. But I do my best to peer. I sniff and dab my eyes.

It was a silly mistake coming upstairs after dinner to fetch a handkerchief, because I felt a bit of a chill coming on. It is decidedly damp in these great rambling Irish houses. 'The people don't want us there,' Philip said when I told him I had never been to Ireland. 'Just you wait, there will be a rebellion. It's only a matter of time.' And he was right. There was trouble in Dublin that Easter just before ... before he ... was killed. I think. I don't truly recall the sequence of things any more ...

And here is Philip's mother now asking me to remember. Demanding that I remember. What did I expect? Wasn't this whole trip about remembering?

It is the last thing I want, of course, to be on my own with Mrs Holt, in this overheated dressing-room of hers, and I knew this had to happen as soon as we arrived at the house and for all of the three days we have been here, I have managed to avoid being alone with her, even when we were out riding, although I don't ride at all well and this upset Mr and Mrs Holt as they had hoped I would like to have Badger, Philip's horse, and take him back to London with me. Anyone could see he's a beautiful horse. I took him a sugar lump yesterday evening. Somehow I think he knew. He just munched the sugar, looking at me.

Anyhow, apart from when I went out to the stable on my own to see Badger, Mummy and Daddy have stayed close, with Mummy and me sleeping in the same room and Daddy making do with the little room the Holts very kindly made available for me—only I am not sure how kind it was really, because it was Philip's room all through his boyhood and how they expected me to sleep in there with all his teddy bears and Boy's Own books and toy engines and things, but I didn't like to say because of course this is Ireland and they do things differently here. And just how differently I didn't know.

Anyhow, the other morning at breakfast Mrs Holt put down her spoon and asked me how I like the view from my window and I just say, 'Oh yes, Mrs Holt, it is such a lovely view,' and say how much I had enjoyed watching the sunrise that morning, and how I must take a walk up that hill before we leave, and she looked at me sharply and said: 'Lucy, you must be mistaken. You cannot possibly see the hill where Philip used to play from your window. You would have to lean out so far to look, you would fall to your death.' Then Mummy, bless her, interrupted and said: 'Oh, Mrs Holt, I believe I can explain. Dear Lucy is not making any mistake or leaning out of windows dangerously, but the confusion arises because we thought it best to rearrange our accommodations ...'

Mrs Holt drew her shawls about herself, as if we had somehow defied carefully thought out arrangements or were behaving like some of her servants, for servants here are often not very helpful I have noticed. They appear to understand orders and then they do things a bit differently and make out they have not understood and you start to think that perhaps you have not instructed them properly and I always get flustered but Mrs Holt gets quite angry with them and makes them do whatever it was all over again. Several times. Like small children.

So anyhow, here she was waiting for me just now as I was about to go back downstairs with the handkerchief and rejoin Mummy and Daddy and Mr Holt for after-dinner drinks. She blocked my way and took advantage of my surprise to draw me in here to her stuffy room and shut the door and say—in that lovely soft voice she has which is definitely not English but is not like the Irish voices of the servants or the men who do the work on the estate, and reminds me suddenly of Philip's voice—'Lucy, it is time you and I had our talk.'

And I sit here with the side of my face burning from the fire, and from properly remembering Philip for the first time, and I say, 'What would you like to know, Mrs Holt?' but my voice sounds very thin and distant and this brings tears to my eyes because I feel cornered and I am not overly sorry about this because I can see the poor woman is upset about her son so I am glad she sees the tears and does not know that I am not crying for Philip, as she supposes, but for myself. Who must now marry Mr Benson whom I met on a London omnibus. The one one three. He has a wine importing business and is doing very well and has grown-up children. His first wife died of diphtheria and his second wife of something else, complications in childbirth I think, and he is hoping it will be a case of third time lucky.

Poor Daddy says it is most unorthodox and Mummy tells him the world has changed and that meeting on a London bus is probably as good a way as any and there isn't the choice of men there used to be. But I don't dare tell Mrs Holt about Roderick Benson. Or the 113 bus.

She pats my shoulder and starts to speak and her voice goes on and on, and there are tears in her voice that I cannot bear so I keep my head down and dab my eyes with my handkerchief that I had luckily fetched before all this. Then she says again: 'Tell me about when the photograph was taken!' She gives me no choice. So I tell her.

'It's not like you think at all, Mrs Holt. Your son Philip was just one of Bertie's friends. Bertie had many friends and whenever any of Bertie's friends were being embarked we would go down to Victoria Station as our patriotic duty, with home-made fruitcake and knitted socks, and anything else we could lay our hands on, to wave goodbye. We kept Union Jack flags by the front door for the purpose.

'That day there was quite a small crowd with Bertie, and one of them, Philip, and I somehow got detached from the rest. There was a photographer's booth set up right where we were standing looking on, while wondering when the train would go as it was already half an hour late, and I asked, for no reason, why didn't he have his picture taken and he said he would, if I would like his picture. Then the photographer who must have overheard him, joined in saying it cost a shilling and the way it worked would be if his name appeared in the KILLED IN ACTION or the WOUNDED, or MISSING AND PRESUMED DEAD lists, copies would be sent to his nearest and dearest with options to purchase more.

'Philip laughed and remarked that this was pretty sharp practice and the man, a short swarthy fellow with hardly any teeth, grinned and said he was only providing a service that would give comfort to loved ones in their time of sorrow. I said, "You must have someone who might like a photograph," and Philip said "There's only Mater and Pater, back in Ballytona—that's the ancestral pile in the middle of nowhere, in the middle of Ireland ..." (Which I think must be when I told him I had never been to Ireland, and he told me there was an uprising coming). "Anyhow, they already have a full length portrait on the wall that was painted for my twenty-first birthday a couple of years back—a clever artist chap came over from Dublin specially—so no, Mater and Pater won't be needing any snap."

'Then the man said, "How about this young lady, then? I am sure Missie here would like a snap." I said, yes I would, and Philip paid the shilling and wrote down the address of the family pile, and I scribbled mine, and he stood to attention while the man disappeared under a black cloth and the picture was taken. I was standing at his side off the set, which is why he is looking to his left. And smiling.

"'If I should die," he said, "it will be nice to think of you having a photo to remember me by."

'Then the whistle for the train began sounding and there was a great commotion up and down the platform and I quite forgot all about it what with one thing and another until a few months later when I received a black-edged envelope in the post and Mummy said, "Do you know what it is, Lucy?" and I said I couldn't think. When I opened it there was a duplicated letter commiserating on my sad loss and enclosing a copy of the Last Picture of the Living. With the word PROOF stamped across his face. And would I like to buy more, without PROOF stamped over them at three shillings a dozen or a bargain five bob for twenty. Which was hardly likely as I had only met the fellow once for about ten minutes on the platform at Victoria Station. Daddy said it was despicable. Mummy said not to let it upset me.

'Then the letters started to arrive. All of them black-edged. With Irish stamps and Irish postmarks. All from Ballytona. Philip's mother—that's you Mrs Holt—had written to the photographers begging for details of when the Last Picture she had also received was taken and who else had been sent proof copies and the photographers had supplied, in consideration of some fee no doubt, my name and address. "Tell us about yourself, Lucy," Mrs Holt had written. And when you said that you hoped "poor Philip" had found love in London before the end, I replied politely that no one could help but love your son. A correspondence ensued, because every time I answered a letter from Ireland, another came back. By return. With all kinds of little gifts— including this pretty lace handkerchief—and invitations to visit.

'You must see, Mrs Holt, thousands upon thousands of men had their photographs taken before they went off to fight. Why is it that *I* have found myself in this unreasonable situation? The war ended years ago. But not for me. The grief-stricken letters from Ireland kept coming, and coming.

'In the end Mummy and Daddy thought the only thing to be done was to visit you as you asked, Mrs Holt. And tell you the truth. They offered to come with me. Which was very sweet of them and is why we are here.

'So, Mrs Holt, the fact is I hardly knew your son, Philip. I didn't even know his name until the duplicated letter came from the photographers. And then you started writing. I had no idea he lived in such a large house built by his ancestors on land given them by King James over two hundred years ago, in return for their support in his conquest of the island. I have never been interested in history. And yes, since you ask, he did kiss me. But only the once, on my gloved hand just as the train was leaving. When I waved him goodbye at Victoria Station, it was not your son I was waving my flag at. I was saying farewell to everyone and everything. And now I am saying goodbye to it all again because I am going to marry Roderick Benson, a man twice my age, who hopes it will be third time lucky and whose youngest daughter is older than me ...'

But Mrs Holt appears not to hear. She weeps and weeps, and then Mummy—who is such a brick and has come to find me and was probably waiting outside the door for this moment—hurries into the room and takes Philip's mother in her arms and says 'Hush, dear Mrs Holt, come with me.' She leads her away which I am jolly glad of and I go over to the window and stand there watching as the two women walk slowly and painfully up the hill—Ballytona Hill—where Philip's children who would have been both their grandchildren would have played.

And I know that Mummy and Mrs Holt with their arms around each other and their heads bent, are talking about Philip, who went Missing in Action on the Somme. They never found him. Or any part of him. And about my brother, Bertie, who ran away under enemy fire and was caught and shot for cowardice at dawn the following morning by his Commanding Officer as an example to the men so naturally we don't like to mention it much.

Then next day, with the Holt family dogs leaping up and barking all around us, our luggage is strapped on to the back of the car and the engine is purring and I can't wait to get away. We thank our hosts for having us and promise to stay in touch although I hardly think this is likely but just as we are about to drive off, Mrs Holt leans right into the back of the car and thrusts the photograph of Philip into my hands and I am about to say I don't want it, but Mummy mouths to me from the front seat to take it. So I do. Which means I now have a copy of Philip's picture without the word PROOF stamped across it. I can see straight into his eyes.

Then we very nearly miss the boat because we are late getting to the quayside in Dublin. Just as we are turning in, and they are about to raise the ramp, a man steps into the street in front of us so that Daddy has to brake violently and as he does so, another man throws a stone at our big English car which luckily bounces off, but it cracks the window right beside me. We keep our nerve. Daddy grips the steering wheel tightly and nearly runs one of the fellows down. We are glad to get parked up in the car deck without further mishap. Mummy says we are not the first of our sort who are happy to be leaving Ireland, and Daddy who is furious about the damage to his paintwork says we won't be the last either.

Anyhow, the crossing back is rough, very rough, and Mummy and Daddy are both ill and luckily have a cabin to themselves to be ill in and I wander the ship which is lurching a lot—which I rather like—and a steward guarding the staircases tells me the commotion I can hear coming from below are the frightened horses who are feeling the waves which makes me glad I left Philip's horse, Badger, behind in Ballytona although it was very nice of the Holts to offer him to me and I did think that maybe I should have accepted, and then sold him in London and got a good price.

When I went to the Ladies to powder my nose, I found the place awash with people of all sorts being ill, and I think what a stout constitution I must have to weather so much storm without mishap. I suddenly feel nauseous being with so many people who can't take the great waves that are really very common on the Irish Sea even in summer so I hurry up on deck, which is thankfully deserted, and I hold on tight to the railing and I pull Philip's photograph out of my pocket. Then I do what I am sure Mrs Holt expected me to.

I tear the Last Picture of the Living into pieces and, before I can toss them over the side, a wave whips the whole lot out of my hand and I see the pieces of the photograph scatter and the salt water wets my cheeks as if tears were falling.

Then I go back down and find the First Class refreshment saloon, which is empty but for one man sitting alone who asks me to join him and share a pot of tea. I do so because I do not think now that I can marry Mr Roderick Benson, the widower I met on the 113 bus.

Thank you, yes. So kind. A splash of milk, please, and two sugars.

The man calls for another cup and saucer to be brought. He pours out my tea himself, adds the milk, and then picks up the silver-plated tongs and neatly plops two cubes of sugar into my cup. He smiles at me a gentle shy smile that reminds me of ... We sit together for a while not speaking, stirring our tea with the funny little soft metal spoons they provide in first class refreshment saloons. The sea is getting rougher if anything and the tea slops a bit and the china rattles but the two of us just sit, laughing lightly and sipping because at this moment, nothing else in the world matters.

THE LEMON PAINTERS

SOMETIMES YOU WRITE A STORY SIMPLY TO PRESERVE a little bit of history that might otherwise be forgotten. Something you alone may know, because of a story passed down in the family perhaps. You also know that unless you take the time to record the details for posterity, this tiny but interesting happening in the past will be lost. Forever. In this case, luckily for me, an artist, the story concerns a tiny but significant bit of art history. And the great artist it deals with is none other than the wonderful Modernist painter, Édouard Manet. He of such masterpieces as *Le Déjeuner sur l'herbe* and *Un bar aux Folies Bergère*. You will more than likely know the pictures even if you don't immediately recognize the titles.

Although I came to live in France during those carefree days when the British could cross the

English Channel and settle themselves anywhere they pleased across Europe—with the same right to do so as a Londoner might decide on the merest whim to move to Hereford or Brighton, Bognor or the Isle of Wight—it happens that I am not the first member of my family to decide they would enjoy life better living in beautiful France. Having met a lot of my fellow expatriates here *en France*, I often wonder if we are not all fleeing something unhappy or unsatisfactory back in 'Blighty', as so many of them call Britain with varying degrees of conscious self-parody. Sometimes with no self-parody at all. Often they are open about the nature of the problem they are evading—a bitter divorce, children not speaking to them, losing a job, a career ending in disappointment or disgrace, sometimes perhaps a collapsed business. Very often you sense, but are not told, a less than perfect family situation. This was certainly the case in the instance I am about to tell you.

My grandfather, who died when I was 14, had had a half brother and sister, both considerably older than himself. His father's first family. I have had to piece together all I recount here from remembered snatches of conversation, and occasional, often whispered, remarks—all made years ago by people who are all now long dead. When I ask my siblings if they can recall anything that might add to my story, they look at me blankly as if I have made it all up. If the details of what I am about to narrate are in places hazy and a little uncertain, the gist of the story has secure foundations.

My grandfather's widow, my paternal grandmother, did not die until I was in my twenties. I used to cycle out to see her and then sit in her damp hillside cottage in Clevedon, with its distant view of Steep Holm in the Bristol Channel, drinking tea and encouraging her to talk to me. She did not need much encouragement. She liked to tell stories about the past. 'It's a shame when things get forgotten, my dear,' she said. I wish now I had taken a tape recorder.

Some things my grandmother recounted—like the missionary aunt burnt alive by Indians in Canada—I regrettably have no way of substantiating. She also told me that my Irish colouring (and that of a couple of cousins) was down to the Irish colleen who had run off with an English soldier billeted in Ireland. This was my grandfather's great grandmother and there was something about her changing her name when she crossed the Irish Sea. My grandmother knew of my artistic aspirations—I usually sat there drawing while she talked, which she said reminded her of my grandfather, and that one of her last memories was of him sitting at the same window making a watercolour of Steep Holm— and it was perhaps because of this she told me in some detail about the lemon painters of Paris, and their association with Édouard Manet. It is this story I want to put on record here. For posterity, as much as for personal reasons, although you can be sure I am very proud of the association. Who wouldn't be?

My grandfather Reginald and his sister Beatrice were born in the last decade of the nineteenth century. An unfortunate time for a boy to come into the world since it meant he would very likely be of an age to fight in the Great War, which was indeed what happened to my grandfather. Buried alive in a trench that caved in on top of his platoon and the only one to emerge alive some ten days later. It wasn't so good for a girl born then either, as all the able-bodied men of her generation were either killed or maimed which somewhat curtailed her life's choices. My great-aunt's boyfriend was killed in the war; when she died in 1981, I acquired a few of her things, enough to prompt me to seek out information about her former beloved when the Records Office at Kew eventually opened the files, and then blurt her sorry story on the front page of the *Daily Telegraph* Saturday supplement, complete with a photograph of her that I had to pinch at random from an old album. My article was published on the last armistice day of the 20th century—my great aunt's story being used to exemplify all the women who had lived out that century deprived of loved ones and so to commemorate the long drawn-out bravery of those who were maimed by the war in a different way.

But this is not about my grandfather and his sister. Their father's first family, also a boy and a girl, had rather astonishingly been born some three decades before them. After their mother died and they inherited a tiny pot of money from her, and after they had fallen out, it seems, with their father who ran a flour mill somewhere in the Bristol area, they had taken themselves off to Paris. They lived very frugally together while they decided what best to do.

Anthony enrolled in some art classes. His sister, Margaret, attended them as well but not as a pupil. She hung about her brother intent on learning all he learnt. Arriving with him at the class, observing as much as she could until everyone in the studio who was not a registered pupil was ordered out. Rather like those announcements when a train is about to leave: 'Will those not intending to travel please make their way to the nearest exit as the train is about to depart.' Even then, Margaret lingered by the doors which she pushed open quietly with her toe so that she could hear the tutor announce the day's exercise.

The brother and sister had selected these art classes with care. You can imagine how Paris was teeming with studios offering lessons to anyone and everyone prepared to pay to learn. There were no end of takers. Among the young ladies were those from America, often with zero talent and not much interest in art, but keen to be able to boast in drawing rooms on their return to Boston or New York that they had 'lifted a paintbrush in Paris'. Henry James very probably wrote a novel about just such a person, for this subject matter was his kind of thing. Then there were young ladies *with* plenty of talent and their Papa's money to spend who came up from the French Provinces, or over from London, Berlin or Stockholm, eager to strike a blow for womanhood and become painters of some renown. Antoine and Margarite, as the brother and sister now called themselves—having sensibly changed their names on the packet-boat halfway across the English Channel—took a keen interest. They were, after all, the children of a prosperous flour mill owner and had grown up with an acute interest in business. They had barely settled into their sparse Montmartre lodgings than they discovered what they had hoped on the voyage over: there was plenty of money to be made in Paris from painting. They saw the sums a certain Auguste Renoir and Edgar Dégas were commanding. They had stood in front of a gallery window in a pretty *passage* and gawked at the price labels. And scoffed. *We can do that!* they said to one another. *Better even!* Hadn't their poor late Mama had them drawing from the moment they could wield a pencil? And bought them a set of watercolours, and later oil paints, as soon as they could use a brush? A thousand francs! For that!

'The gallery probably takes a big cut,' Antoine observed.

'Even so!'

On the strength of this discovery, they treated themselves to cups of frothing *chocolat chaud* and even went so far as to pay extra to have little mountains of *crème fouetée* floating on top. 'I think you should take some of our paintings and tour the galleries first thing tomorrow,' Margarite said. 'I will stay at home and do some more.'

The pair knew that if they were to make a life for themselves in Paris, there was no time to be lost. Their mother's money would not last for ever. On the way home they visited an art shop and spent a sizeable chunk of it on the smartest portfolio they could find, with brass embossed corners and ribbons to secure their pictures elegantly inside. The next morning Antoine left their lodgings with this large and now bulging object awkwardly tucked under his arm. Margarite leaned out of the window as far as she could and watched her brother struggling along the street below. Then, for the first time since they had arrived in Paris, she took up her paintbrush. Spurred on by the thought of that thousand francs, she spent the day painting the floor to ceiling window and the light beyond, fashioning a charming but rather empty interior. I could put a figure in it later, she thought. Perhaps their mother sewing, done from memory. Or Antoine smoking. He could sit in the empty chair that evening while he described his adventures in the *passages*—oh, how she hoped he succeeded!

It was a long day for Margarite. Each time she heard the heavy door down below open and close her ears pricked up. Occasionally footsteps could be heard mounting the stairs. Once or twice she even went out on the landing to call down to her brother but each time she saw a shadowy figure disappearing into one of the *appartements* below. Once a man in a top hat looked up, and even called to her something in French; she had hurried back into their rooms and she saw in the mirror that she had blushed an unpleasant shade of scarlet that did not in any way become her. She resolved not to pop out when she heard someone else returning home. The day dragged. She had finished her painting (she worked fast) and started another and was dozing off when the door eventually opened and Antoine appeared. He threw the new portfolio down on the chair and stood before his sister sighing.

'Well?' she said, barely able to suppress her excitement.

'It was no good,' he said. 'We might just as well have saved ourselves the expense of the new portfolio.'

Margarite was nonplussed. 'Whatever happened?' Perhaps, after all, she should have been the one to sally forth and do the rounds of the galleries. Hadn't that little place in Bath near the bridge taken the watercolour robin she had been working on at the time of their mother's death? She had smiled at the pompous man who ran the place and he told her he would probably take anything else she cared to bring him for he thought she had a very special touch with her brush. By then, though, brother and sister had resolved to try their luck in Paris. 'Did they *look* at our paintings?'

'They looked all right! Oh, Maggie, just let me get my coat off.' She had never seen her brother so downhearted.

'Perhaps you didn't try the right places. There are so many galleries in Paris, all we have to do is find one that likes our style.'

'If only it were that easy. Look, could you make some tea. I'm completely parched. Then I will tell all.'

Antoine glanced at her easel. And then at the more finished picture on the floor. He shook his head. She was disappointed. Silently she filled the copper kettle from the pitcher on the washstand and lit the candle stove underneath. She took their teapot down from its hook and measured out a small spoonful of tea. Her brother sat with his back to her, his young shoulders miserably hunched. She put one of the little tea biscuits she had bought in a *pâtisserie* the day before on a plate but when she placed this and his tea at his elbow he did not notice.

'What exactly was the problem, Tony?' she asked.

He did not reply. She saw him look over at her long and hard and decide not to speak.

'You had better tell me,' she said.

'You won't want to hear. We may as well pack up and go back home.'

'Nonsense! Whatever can they have said to make you so despondent? Really Tony, dear, this is so unlike you I am scared. You will have to tell me sometime. Tell me now!'

'All right, Mags. But as I said, you won't want to hear. I went back to that gallery we saw the first day we were here. With those pictures of brightly coloured fruit and dancers in the window. I asked the man inside if I could speak to the proprietor. He laughed at my bad French and said he was the proprietor. I explained why I had come. I opened the portfolio and ...'

'And?'

'He laughed again but this time at my paintings!'

'No!'

'Yes, and yours too. As we agreed, I did not make a distinction. He quickly ran his hands through them all and laughed again. He said the fine new portfolio was worth more than all our pictures put together!'

'How rude! Are you sure he wasn't laughing from happiness that you were proposing selling them to him?' Margarite asked, mystified by what her brother was telling her. No one had ever laughed at their work before. Hadn't they both had pictures in the Bristol Academy of Fine Arts Summer Exhibition just about every year since they were 14 and 15? And had they not on several occasions been awarded certificates, once or twice even taking silver and bronze medals?

'He was laughing that I had the audacity to show my work to him, let alone expect him to purchase it. My French may not be good, Maggie, but I understood his meaning very clearly.'

Margarite was genuinely taken aback. 'Perhaps our style did not suit him ...'

'Our style—as you choose to politely call it—does not suit Paris! After that awful encounter, I tied up the portfolio again as neatly as I could—I could have done with your nimble fingers because to tell the truth, I was so shaken by all he had said (and there was a great deal more than I have told you, but all to the same derisive effect) I decided to call at every gallery I came across who would open their doors to me. First off, a woman who assured me her gallery was the best in Paris ...'

'A woman?'

'I was surprised too. She had some aristocratic title—de something, de something else—which I have wiped from my memory. I untied the badly tied ribbon and she only looked at the first picture—your painting of the Clifton Suspension Bridge at dawn, as it happened. She told me to retie the portfolio immediately. '*Thees* are of no interest!' she said in bad English for she had worked out my nationality at once and spoke with something of a hiss. 'I am expecting'—and she mentioned a name I have also now forgotten but she spoke it with great awe. 'He is the most important collector in Paris. I have no time at present ...'

Naturally I offered to return at a more convenient moment.

'*Non!*' she said. 'It will be no good. Your work is unschooled. You are not trained. I do not even look at work where the artist has not attended at least ten years at the *Académie*. And even then, I expect something remarkable.'

'You could have mentioned the Bristol Academy of Fine Arts!' Margaret said lamely. They were very much Margaret and Anthony again at that moment.

Her brother laughed bitterly. 'I don't think so,' he said.

'But there were other galleries? You have been out all day ...'

'I have been out all day visiting those other galleries. And believe you me, it's hopeless. They all found fault—all those who agreed to look at our pictures, that is. And they all said much the same thing. Some of them asked outright where I had trained. Of course I mumbled about colleges in England. They didn't listen. They insisted on knowing if I was attached to any *atelier*—that's French for studio by the way—here in Paris, and I had to admit I was not. Several of them said they would look again at my work when I had done at least a year or two in an *atelier*—a studio—here.'

'Well, that was good, wasn't it? Wasn't it?'

Again, Anthony laughed bitterly.

'You have lost heart, I see.'

'No, Mags, don't try and tell me it will all work out. It won't. Paris is not like Bristol, or even London. Do you remember that print studio in Cornhill that took a few of your sketches and gave us cash on the spot ...'

'I am *not* going back to England.'

'Neither am I. We will have to do whatever it takes.'

'If we need to attach ourselves to some artist's studio and pay him for a few lessons so that we look as if we have been taught by him and the galleries can charge for our work because of the association ...'

Antoine brightened. His sister had completely grasped the situation.

' ...then that is what we will do. I dare say it will be expensive. These Parisian artists will no doubt know how to charge.'

'They will know they can take advantage of us foreigners. That is for sure ...'

'We will just have to live very carefully to preserve our money.'

'Paris is certainly expensive. That *chocolat chaud* ...'

'We will have to forgo *chocolat chaud* until we are making money ...'

'And then we will enjoy *chocolat chaud* with *crème fouetée* on top every morning for breakfast. I hear this fellow Manet is raking it in!'

'It is only a matter of time, Tony dear, before we too are "raking it in",' Margarite laughed.

The brother and sister quickly set about looking for a studio that would provide the necessary lessons. As they had predicted, classes were expensive. No one would negotiate a reduction in the fees because there were two of them. It quickly became clear that their happy image of themselves painting side by side at easels in a professional studio was an impossible dream. Margarite had pictured the pair of them producing such amazingly beautiful work that dealers who came to speak to their tutor would spot the pictures on their easels and speak to them as well, if not instead! Her daydreams were soon crushed, if not altogether shattered.

'I am thinking that perhaps it would be better if only you went to the classes, Tony. I will come with you, and come back to fetch you. I will bring you some lunch and sit and eat with you. I will learn whatever there is to be learnt alongside you but without the expense.'

'That might work.'

'It must be made to work.'

It did not altogether work. The first painting class Antoine attended, at a studio belonging to Édouard Manet, Margarite stayed with her brother as long as she felt she reasonably could without anyone suspecting that she was not merely there to support her brother in his artistic ambitions. The tutor announced the students were to work on a *nature morte*. He also said that *maître* Manet would very likely call by later perhaps to see how they were getting on.

'Dead nature?' Antoine queried in a whisper.

'It's French for what we call a still life,' Margarite replied.

'Please could all escorts and anyone accompanying students leave the atelier at once. Classes are about to commence,' the tutor's assistant cried out, appalled that the English should come and disrupt proceedings by crowding round the easels and talking in whispers together. Margarite fled. But not before her brother had suggested that he would make his own way home at the end of the day.

'But your lunch?' She asked

'I will go without. I don't need lunch,' Antoine said.

Margarite walked back to their lodgings sadly. Things were not working out how she had hoped. At least Antoine was in a room full of other artists, working at an easel, hopefully learning something. She fetched her sketchbook and decided to walk to the park ...

And so began weeks that turned into months that all contained days and days that were all more or less the same. Only on Sundays did brother and sister spend time together. On one such Sunday, perhaps on a boat they had hired but perhaps not—they were avidly saving their *francs*, after all, or *napoleons* as they had learned to call the coins—Margarite asked when she was likely to see any of her brother's endeavours. She herself had sketchbooks full of people she had seen in the various *parcs* around Paris where she had spent her lonely days.

'Never!' cried her brother. 'They make us tear our work up at the end of the day.'

'What?' Margarite was taken aback.

'It's the studio rule. Strictly enforced by the assistants.'

'I don't believe it!' Margarite exclaimed though of course she believed her brother implicitly. 'How can they have such a rule when you ... I mean, we, of course—are paying so much for the privilege of your being there.'

'It's the way it is.'

'Why didn't you say so before?'

'I didn't like ... I knew you wouldn't like it.'

'I don't! I thought that at least you would have some new work to show in the portfolio.'

'I thought so too. The first day I accepted it as the accepted practice of the studio. I assumed they didn't want people to see students' trial runs, as it were. But as I got better and better—and I do wish you could see the bowl of fruit I was painting this week ...'

'A bowl of fruit! You were painting a bowl of fruit the first day.'

'I thought I might be able to bring it home. As a point of fact, I actually asked. I said that you would like to see it but the assistant, a cruel little weasel of a man called Julien, grabbed hold of my painting and tore it from corner to corner. He opened the stove and crammed it in before I could so much as protest. All I could do was stand there gazing at the flame that sprang up and gobbled my masterpiece ... I was so upset I very nearly burst into tears and would have done if I hadn't been determined this Julien would not have the satisfaction. I never was very good at keeping a stiff upper lip, as mother always told us to ...'

'She did, didn't she!' Margarite said fondly. Whatever would Mother have said if she knew that they had almost spent up nearly all the money she had left them to secure their independence and were no further forward in establishing themselves as the artists they so badly wanted to be. The artists she had so badly wanted them to be, despite their father the flour merchant's more down to earth ambitions for them.

Obviously, he remarried later on and created another family, hoping for a son who would take over the flour mill. As it happened my grandfather, especially after his trauma in the trenches, was no better suited to the flour milling business than his stepbrother had been. The mill went bankrupt in the thirties. There was some talk that he had been defrauded by a smooth-talking business partner. But that was years later ...

In the middle of that night, after much tossing and turning in their little narrow beds on either side of their tiny attic bedroom, separated off for the sake of privacy by a sheet suspended from the ceiling, Margarite called out to her brother: 'Are you awake?'

She was pretty sure he must be, because she knew he was as restless as she.

'Yes,' came his voice from the other side of the sheet.

'OK,' she said. 'Light a candle, Tony. I have a plan.'

Antoine's heart leapt. Margarite's plans were always good. And this one, when she described it to him, was as good as any she had ever come up with.

If the pair of them had come to Paris and encountered such difficulties establishing themselves as artists—even with all their experience and talents, those certificates and medals from the Bristol Academy, not to mention pooling their resources and eking them out so carefully—then they could not be the only ones. What of all those American heiresses who wanted to return to New York and Boston boasting that they had learnt to paint in Paris? What of that girl from Oslo who had told them how impossibly dark it was in winter back home, months and months of the year when you could hardly see to paint? And as for all the slightly overweight and overdressed young ladies from the French provinces who were

all homesick and had little talent but hoped for
... Not to mention their fellow countrymen and
women who flocked over the English Channel as
they themselves had done ....

'What of them all?' Her brother asked, barely
able to contain his excitement.

'We will organize a school for them. '

'Us?'

'We will make it easy for them all to part with
their money. We will offer a six week course in
painting fruit. You will repeat everything *maître*
Manet has told you.'

'*Maître* Manet has hardly ever visited and
when he did, he took no notice of us at all and we
were expressly forbidden to speak to him.'

'That is absurd when you were paying.'

'I know, but it is a rule rigorously enforced
by the dreadful Julien and his equally dreadful
assistant whose name I can never remember.'

'Jean, you once said.'

'Yes, that's it. Jean!'

'Forget them. There will be no talking in our
classes either. A rule I shall enforce as rigorously
as any weasel faced Julien or Jean. We will offer
six weeks of expert tuition by a painter personally
taught by *maître* Manet—who seems to be all the
fashion at the moment—and that painter, of
course, is you!'

'Me? Well, I suppose that is technically true.'

'You will teach everything you have gleaned
from his *atelier*, and anything else you can think

of besides. And since, as far as I can tell, you have spent nearly six months learning how to paint still lives—*natures mortes*!—that is all we ourselves will offer. I will go out at the crack of dawn each morning and buy lots of fruit.'

'Sometimes we have spent whole days painting lemons. Lemons, lemons and nothing but lemons. I did not like to tell you ...'

'So much the better. I shall buy every pupil a lemon every other day at two centimes each. You will tell them that painting lemons is the very best way to learn. "As *maître* Manet says", you will repeat—and often— "once you have mastered *le citron* you can paint anything!" All we need do is find some premises.'

'That won't be easy.'

'What do you think I have been doing all the time you have been sequestered with *maître* Manet learning nothing ....'

'I reckon he must have another studio somewhere, where he actually does his painting.'

'In *our* art school you will be present the whole time. Our students will get their money's worth. And more. Anyhow, as I said, I have wandered the streets of Paris more assiduously than any of the girls this place is apparently so famed for ...'

'Margaret!'

'Margarite, if you please! Madame Margarite, if I am to run our school! I know exactly the place. Give me a day or two and I will have secured the lease ...'

'We don't have much money left.'

'All the more reason to get on with it, at once.'

And so they did. *L'École Anglaise de Peinture*, housed in a curious warehouse with perfect north light, was soon so popular brother and sister became very fussy about whom they admitted as pupils. These needed to be so untalented that even the ability to paint a lemon reasonably well would constitute a vast achievement to them. Ateliers across Paris quickly suffered. The number of eager students wanting to train in them dried up. *L'École Anglaise* and its six week course in *nature morte* became the rage.

One afternoon, maître Manet enquired of his assistants, Julien and Jean, what was going on. Revenue from the classes that they were superintending in one of his lesser studios had entirely plummeted. His other studios were practically empty also. 'It's that young English fellow,' he was told. 'The one who showed up at first with his sister snooping round ...'

'Oh?'

'We didn't mention it at the time. We just told her to go away and not come back. Anyhow, from what we can make out, the pair of them have now set up an art school of their own in Montmartre and are gathering up all the talentless would-be artists with funds. We cannot compete.'

Maître Manet decided to pay the upstart English painting school a visit and put them right about one or two things. As soon as he arrived,

Margarite knew exactly who he was. He swept past her as she sat at her little reception desk reckoning up the accounts and stood at the glass door of one of the studios. He then went to the glass door of the other studio. He was astonished. Every pupil, at least thirty in each room, was hard at work painting a lemon.

'This is madness,' he said. 'A whole school of painting teaching nothing at all but how to paint lemons. You are *complètement fou*, you English!'

Margarite laughed. 'Too right,' she said in her best French. '*Complètement fou* we may be, but it is making us the money we could not make in Paris from our own paintings, maître Manet. And since my brother didn't learn much, despite paying the high fees you charge to train at your celebrated *atelier*, we are at least putting what little he did learn to good use.'

Manet snorted—the artist was famous for his snorts—and went back to his principal studio and in a fit of temper—he was also famous for his fits of temper—dashed off the exquisite *Le Citron* that now hangs in the Musée d'Orsay. A painting that did indeed inaugurate a whole craze for painting lemons in Paris, known in art history as *citromania* (or *citromanie*, in France). 'If you can't beat them, join them,' he muttered, or the French to that effect. This turn of events was most gratifying, of course, to my grandfather's stepbrother and stepsister, as all the pupils at their *L'École Anglaise* felt themselves at the very cutting edge of the latest fashion. In painting. In Paris. They were able to return to New York, Boston, London, Berlin and Oslo or go back to the French provinces from whence they had come and boast that they themselves had been taught to paint lemons by a man who had trained with the man who started an entire art movement. *Le citromanie*.

'If the family only had one of those Manet lemons,' my grandmother said wistfully, 'think how rich we might be.'

'I think we are pretty rich anyway,' I told her. 'There isn't anyone in the family not capable of executing a competent lemon!'

She laughed and said that when I was older, I would probably agree that the money might have come in handy. 'Such a shame your grandfather did not keep up with his step siblings. By the time I met him, they were long gone.'

A couple of months ago, I finished writing this and sent it to my brother—as the only other person she might have told the story to—for comment. I heard nothing back from him so I telephoned and asked if he had received it. 'Oh yes,' he said vaguely. 'I saw you sent some papers, but I've been very busy recently. I haven't had a chance to take a look. In fact, I am not at all sure where the envelope is now.'

'Can you find it please, and read it, and let me know if you have anything to add,' I asked. He sighed heavily, said again that he was very busy unlike me with time to spare scribbling stories, but then agreed somewhat ungraciously to do as I asked.

A week or so later my envelope came back to me, sellotaped up rather badly and with his address in my handwriting crossed out and my address untidily written over it. Insufficient postage had been added and I had to pay a fee at the local post office to take delivery. The papers inside were scrunched up as if he had stuffed them back in the envelope in a temper. Scrawled at the end of my story, in writing I took a long time to decipher, he had written: 'It wasn't Manet, you idiot, but Monet. And it wasn't lemons they were all painting at that pokey art school above the hairdressers (and before you ask, yes, I once had a photo of it, long since lost) but irises. Monet was famous for his irises. I'd have thought you, of all people, knew that! It was *you* that spent a whole weekend the summer after your A-levels doing nothing but painting lemons. Lemon after lemon. How we laughed. I do think, Charlotte— as you call yourself now!—if you are going to write stories about the family, you might at least get your facts right.'

Next time I visit the Musée D'Orsay, I am going to buy a postcard of Manet's beautiful lemon, and send it to him without a stamp.

POSTCARDS
CHASING CHÂTEAUX I

ACROSS THE TABLE, MR HUTTON FROWNED AND solemnly shook his head. 'You can certainly *buy* postcards of most of the nearby châteaux,' he informed the girls ponderously, wiping the sides of his mouth with his napkin and smiling condescendingly at them as he did so. He took a loud sip from his wine glass. And then continued. 'I notice they have a fair selection on offer in the foyer here, if it's postcards you want!'

'Well, no,' said Laura. 'We were actually hoping to visit ...'

'All of them pre-war, of course, as re-photographing the places has hardly been a priority with the authorities. As you can imagine, what with some of them left in a shocking state by the departing Hun. I gather the Boche used any ancestral portrait left on the walls for target practice. Centuries-old paintings turned into worthless pin cushions!' He laughed rather gleefully at the notion of valuable art destroyed in this fashion.

Isabel and Laura winced. The one thing they had been told by just about everyone they had spoken to before coming to France was never to mention the war. Whatever else you do, or say, never ever mention the Germans. You cannot imagine the sensitivity of people who have been occupied, all of them having found themselves on one side or the other and now having to live together again. So much easier for us, being bombed and hating them! And now here was Mr Godfrey Hutton, a man they had only encountered for the first time the other day in this same hotel dining room, pointing his fork at them and loudly mentioning both the war and the Germans, at their table! They glanced at their step-mother but Eleanor either hadn't heard or was entirely unconcerned. She was meekly and unenthusiastically working her way through her meal. Her mind, as usual, elsewhere.

'And you will no doubt pay at least double for them here than the exact same postcards sell for down in the village,' Mr Hutton continued, still jabbing the air with his fork, 'but the extra expense will save you the bother of going out.'

'But we are here to go out!' Laura protested with an impatient shake of her head. Why, oh why, did these bores always latch on to them, she wondered impatiently glancing round the hotel dining room. There had been that man on the cross-Channel ferry who insisted on offering them 'something stronger' while they were buying their cups of tea and then came and sat with them while they were drinking those cups of tea. And then that man at the station in Paris who had offered to help with their baggage and wouldn't leave them alone, so that they had had the devil of a job shaking him off. But at least those men had been good looking. Quite handsome, in fact. And French. Whereas this dreadful bore was English and had three chins! Why couldn't he have taken his three chins and gone and sat with someone else and driven them crazy instead with his tedious conversation!

'Which, I suppose, when you think about it, is precisely the point of hotel kiosks.'

'Is it?' Isabel asked wonderingly.

'What point?' Laura was sharp and far less polite.

'Why, to save clientele all the bother and danger of having to venture into the outside world.' Mr Hutton chuckled. He then popped a small potato into his mouth and, still chomping on it, so that they could see it going round and round in his mouth like something in a spin drier, he continued his theme: 'Yes, my dears, I think you will find that, by and large, you will not be able to actually visit any châteaux round here. Their owners, the Marquises and Counts, all got discouraged trying to hold crumbling bricks and mortar together. They have long since packed up and gone away.'

'Not visit the châteaux!' Isabel gaped at Laura who frowned. Wasn't this the reason they were here? It was Isabel's turn to glance round the dining room at *tous les Anglaises* bent silently over their plates, pretending not to be listening in when they were all clearly agog. No one else was speaking. How she hated them! She had agreed to come with Laura and Eleanor on this jaunt to escape the uncle and aunt who had tried to inveigle her into spending the summer holiday with them and now here she was, stuck in a drab hotel dining room packed full of uncles and aunts. *And* this frightful Mr Hutton! 'I thought that that was why we were all of us here! For the châteaux. I assumed ... I mean, what else can there be to do in these parts?' So far, she had only seen cows and fields, and there wasn't exactly a shortage of them back in England.

Mr Hutton now glanced round the room also. He laughed dismissively. 'Eat nice meals—even if they are a bit...' he grimaced at his plate. 'Well, not so nice. There is nothing grand about the beef at the Grand Bœuf!' He laughed at his own joke.

Isabel opened her mouth to say something but thought better of it.

Laura, though, said, 'I always understood French food was meant to be ...'

Mr Hutton ignored them. 'Well, of course, there is the local wine. Which isn't at all bad. If you like that kind of thing. The Loire Valley is, as you must already know, my dears, famous for its superb vintages. You can also soak up the sun. When there is any. What else do you expect to do in France? Or on holiday, for that matter. In point of fact, my late wife, Mary, and I made a point of coming here, to the Grand Hôtel du Bœuf, for a couple of weeks every year ...'

'How nice!' murmured Eleanor vaguely.

'Here!' said Isabel. 'Every year?'

'Yes, here!' Godfrey Hutton smiled.

'But why? There must be hundreds, thousands, of other hotels across France to visit. Some of them much nicer ...'

Laura wished from the depths of her heart that Izzie would not encourage the dreadful man. If they stopped replying he would eventually get the message and shut up. And hopefully sit somewhere else tomorrow.

If Mr Hutton sensed any criticism of his good person, he was unperturbed. 'You may be right, young lady,' he said. 'I am sure, as you say, there are plenty of other establishments. But the Grand Hôtel du Bœuf suited Mary and me. Smart enough but not too smart. Plenty of other English, which makes life easy. Although, of course, the place is not at all what it was when we first came to France. But then, nowhere is. How could it be after five years occupied by the

Germans? Did you know the Frenchies call them the Alboche—which is a mixture of allemande and cabbage.'

'How do you know all these things?' Isabel asked, almost admiringly.

'Did you know that the word grenade comes from the French for pomegranate?'

'Well, you would hardly expect *anywhere* to be the same after five years,' Laura paused, and gave a little gulp, 'whatever had, um, taken place.' Laura couldn't imagine why their stepmother had permitted the man—let alone invited him!—to sit at their table.

He is on his own, Eleanor had whispered, it's only kind. Almost immediately the sisters had realized that there was a very good reason why this man was on his own. The other diners had been at the Grand Hôtel du Bœuf longer than them and had evidently wised up to the man. They had all cleverly made sure any spare chairs were instantly removed from their tables so it was scarcely possible for anyone to join them. In any case, it was all very well for their stepmother. She simply made no effort. She left them to it. She left them to Godfrey Hutton. It was a shame to have gone to all the effort of coming here, and then this happens.

'As I was saying,' Mr Hutton pointed his fork again, this time at Laura, 'you will be able to purchase a full set of pre-war postcards of all the nearby châteaux at the hotel reception. At least they can't charge you extra for the stamps—though I dare say they would if they could but luckily the value is printed on the stamps—*timbres de poste*, by the way—and that will also save you the bother going out and finding a post office. It's a dreadful trek on unkempt tracks and when you get there, its full of ... well, Frenchmen! You girls need to be careful. A few years ago, there was an incident involving an entirely innocent Englishwoman down in the village ...'

'An "incident"?' Izzie was immediately interested but Mr Hutton clearly felt he had said enough. He nodded his head grimly at the recollection.

'I don't want to alarm you,' he told them. 'Far be it from me to wreck your holiday in any way, but forewarned is very definitely forearmed.' He then set about applying himself once more to his dinner.

Laura frowned at her own neglected plate and started slicing the strange piece of vegetable swimming in the richly flavoured sauce. She had pushed the stringy meat to one side. She did not dare glance at her sister and step-mother but she was acutely aware out of the corner of her eye that their knives and forks were stilled. They were not enjoying themselves. She felt responsible. Visiting châteaux had been *the very reason* she had been so insistent on coming to this little place they had none of them heard of before because it had stated—unequivocally—

in the guidebook she had consulted with such frequency and pleasure over the long strange winter, that 'the Grand Hôtel du Bœuf must be the perfect base for châteaux visiting. An unusual concentration of some of France's lesser known, but most exquisite examples of these beautifully preserved historic edifices, many with admirable gardens that can often be enjoyed for a modest recompense ...' Unfortunately she had left the deceitful guidebook back at home in the mansion flat in Paddington which was a shame as she would like to find the page and wave it at Mr Hutton. Not that he was the sort of man one could imagine waving anything at.

She turned now to her step-mother but Eleanor only smiled sadly at something beyond them all in the far distance. She wore the distracted air she had adopted when their father died and had worn ever since. Visiting châteaux had not been her idea of a holiday—not now, not ever again, not without dear Alfred!—but for the sake of peace, since Laura really had been ridiculously insistent and Isabel had been keen to get away. Poor lovelorn Isabel, besotted with the boy next door and sobbing her heart out when he had suddenly gone and married someone else. Eleanor made no attempt to engage in conversation with Mr Hutton despite the fact that she had waved him to the empty chair at their table in the mistaken belief, apparently, that he might be entertainment—or, at least, company—for them.

And hadn't she told Laura and Isabel, right back at the start when they had first suggested she accompany them on this outlandish excursion, that she would not join them in sight-seeing or any other holiday activity. It was simply not her thing. Not anymore. Once she had enjoyed little excursions to historic spots with their father but that part of her life was over. Forever. Yes, she would sit happily enough on her own in the gardens of whichever hotel they chose and think melancholy thoughts and soak up *le soleil*. 'I shall wear my new black straw hat.'

'And if there was no "*soleil*"? Laura had asked anxiously. 'Supposing it rains all the time?'

'Then so much the better. I shall merely set myself up in the drawing room—the lounge—the *entresol* or whatever this particular establishment calls its public rooms, and I shall thumb my way through old magazines. And read the odd novel. Do my knitting. Do very little, in fact. And leave you both to chase your châteaux. Let it never be said that I have in any way got in the way of poor Alfred's dear girls.' She had clutched Laura's hand and squeezed it encouragingly.

'You have always been very kind, Eleanor,' Laura had said.

The dining room bore had eaten his *plât du jour* and was now busily mopping up the remains of the sauce with some bread. He shook his head again at poor Alfred's dear girls. 'Yes, indeed. It's a well-known fact the guidebooks lure you here with promises of untold châteaux opportunities in the vicinity, but in reality ...' Mr Hutton popped a piece of bread dripping with sauce into his mouth, licked his fingers, and forgot to finish his sentence.

So Laura made a collection. As if in defiance of Godfrey Hutton, she went straight to the hotel foyer after dinner and bought one of every card they had. Her sister, Isabel, said 'She has no choice. She brought us here to see châteaux and we are to see them, it seems, even if only on postcards! Pre-war government issue postcards at that!'

Eleanor laughed but her laughter was in no way malicious. She never took sides. Never had. Never would. She had loved their father. He had died. And the girls were his daughters. She accepted them as a fact of life. And gave them no thought. They could, and must, look after themselves.

Laura walked down to the village in the morning and returned having purchased a rather functional notebook to stick the postcards in, and a pot of glue with which to do so. She arrived back in time to avoid a dramatic downpour. The heavens opened just as she sailed through the front door. The concierge laughed. 'You timed that well,' he said.

'I'm Laura,' she told him, holding out her hand.

'Philippe,' he said. 'Philippe Denzat. At your service. If there is anything I can do to make your stay more comfortable ...'

'Well, thank you, Monsieur Philippe,' Laura said. Then she found an empty table in the crowded *entresol*—for the rain had put an end to any possibility of outdoor activities that day— and she spread her postcards out and began gluing them extravagantly into her notebook. 'Collage,' she explained gleefully to the amusement of the other guests. 'The French for glue is *colle* and so, *eh bien, je fais la collage!*'

'*Le collage!*' some know-all corrected her. 'It's *le garage. Le fromage.* But *la plage, la cage* and *la page.* Those are the only exceptions. French is quite complicated you know.'

'Impossible stuff,' someone else joined in.

'That's why I never speak it,' another guest hiding behind an old newspaper agreed. 'Bound to get into a muddle, what with all those irregular verbs.'

'Why everyone can't just learn English! It would make life so much simpler.'

'Yes, but half the fun of coming here, to France that is, is to have a go,' said Laura, dabbing at the back of one of her *carte postales* with her glue brush.

Isabel was annoyed at her sister making an exhibition of herself. But it did not end there. The weather brightened up that afternoon, by which time Laura had acquired the use of a bicycle. She had been chatting to her friend Philippe— Monsieur Denzat to everyone else—who had sold her the postcards. He had helped her make sure she had one of each. He had even thrown in a few extra he found on the shelf under his counter. He had said, although she didn't altogether understand, that he found her enthusiasm for this quiet part of the Loire Valley refreshing. Other visitors tended to come because it was less dramatic, less touristy, and therefore cheaper. To have a young and very attractive guest who had positively chosen the area was a pleasure. It then turned out his son was away on military service and Laura was very welcome to borrow the boy's bicycle.

Isabel was outraged. 'You can't go borrowing some soldier's bicycle!'

'I am not borrowing it, I am paying a few francs rent for the use of it.'

'It's far too big and heavy for you: you are bound to fall off. And in any case, English ladies do not go cycling round the French countryside on their own, on rented bicycles. It's ... looking for trouble!'

'Why don't you see if you can rent one too, Izzie. Come and "look for trouble" with me!'

Isabel huffed and muttered and then she did try to speak to Monsieur Denzat herself, but got nowhere. He put his head first on one side and then the other, smiled quizzically and twisted the pointed ends of his extravagant moustache. Then he emphatically shook his head. There was only *une bicyclette* available for miles around, Monsieur Denzat indicated by stretching his arms wide to make the point, and Mademoiselle Laura had nabbed it. Or words to that effect.

Next Isabel tried to get the bicycle confiscated. 'She'll come a cropper,' she told their step-mother. 'She'll twist an ankle or break a leg and then what will we do? How will we ever get back to Calais? And the ferry, I mean, those gangplanks were steep ...'

Eleanor laughed gently. She had no powers over Laura, she said, absenting herself behind an old copy of *Country Life*. Oh, the lovely houses. So prettily English. She glanced at the girls, who were both English but not by any stretch of the imagination particularly pretty, and wondered at the turn of events. Home was now a cavernous apartment in a mansion block in Paddington that had been inhabited by poor dear Alfred and his previous wife, the girls' mother, and which she now shared with these squabbling sisters who only acknowledged her presence or any sort of authority when they called on her to settle their childish quarrels. Why had she supported Laura in her desperate desire to come château hunting? Simply to shut the younger girl up, she supposed. And as for Izzie, who had needed such copious comforting when that spotty youth whose mother lived on the floor below had unceremoniously dumped her. Telling her, apparently, as he did so, that she resembled a horse. Within a fortnight he had married someone else and Izzie was stuck in the flat, unable to go out in case she encountered him and his bride on the stairwell. Yes, Eleanor was very grateful to the kind Mr Hutton for taking it on himself to entertain the pair.

Isabel next insisted on 'having a turn'. She seized the bicycle from her sister and rode it furiously down the hotel driveway, determined to wreck the confounded machine. This proved harder than she imagined. When she and it collided with one of the chestnut trees that grew so elegantly either side of the drive, it was not the bicycle she wrecked. The doctor came from the village, a Dr Denzat, cousin of the hotel concierge, it turned out. He spoke voluble French, prodded her all over and then—with a lot more prodding—strapped up her ankle tightly and injected some strong painkiller into her arm. 'You weel be all-right,' he said. Consigned therefore to one of the sofas in the hotel's *entresol*, poor Isabel was forced to do something that did not come naturally to her in all her dealings with her younger sister: she had to admit defeat. Luckily Mr Hutton came to the rescue. He took to coming and sitting beside her each day, puffing at his pipe and reading out snippets from the English newspapers (of a few weeks back) for Monsieur Denzat saw no need to buy papers since there were always plenty left behind by departing guests. The crosswords already filled in. Sometimes incorrectly. Odd pieces had been snipped out rendering articles on the reverse frustratingly incomplete and incomprehensible.

Hutton grunted at this and Isabel sympathized. Why had a certain Mr Henry Bishopston, 43, of Riverside Road, Croydon murdered his wife and buried her, together with her pet canaries, under the floorboards? 'The police courts heard evidence from a lodger ...' and that was it. They would never know what the lodger had had to say. Then what of the boy, Ginger something, who had been caught stowing away on a flight from Hendon to the Arctic circle. He had been strapped to a parachute and ejected from the rear of the aircraft into the sea off Aberdeen. His widowed mother had taken herself to Downing Street where .... Isabelle and Mr Hutton passed the time filling in the gaps. Ginger had swum to the nearest lighthouse on the back of a seal. The lodger had seen Mrs Bishopston sneaking out of the house with her fancy man, a vendor of birdseed.

Laura, meanwhile, took her notebook filled with its somewhat haphazardly glued-in postcards and popped it into the pretty basket Mr Denzat— Philippe, to her—had procured from somewhere and attached to the front of her bicycle by means of an old scarf. She had borrowed a detailed map of the area from Dr Denzat, that cousin who took to calling regularly at the hotel and touching Isabelle far more than either she or Mr Hutton deemed necessary, eventually pronouncing his patient first 'out of danger' and then 'on the mend'. Every morning while the hotel guests were breakfasting, Laura cycled away down the driveway, her skirts flapping prettily around her. Everyone paused—mid-boiled egg and skimpily buttered toast soldiers—to watch until she was out of sight.

Isabel shuddered at the way her sister was making such a spectacle of herself. And in front of Mr Hutton. 'My wife had a younger sister,' he told her. 'Poor Mary. Bane of her life, was Joyce.'

'I wouldn't really say Laura was the bane of my life,' Izzie laughed.

The first château she tracked down, the nearest, was visible from the road but the wire fence the other side of a deep ditch that ran all around the fields surrounding it proved impenetrable. She reluctantly gave up and moved on to the next. The next one turned out to not even be visible, try as she might to locate it, circling and circling a few gravelly tracks where she could find no one at all to help her. The third château was also well hidden but this time the gate was open. There were signs up saying *Interdit de* and *Offense à* etc but these signs were everywhere in this part of France, she decided, and therefore meant nothing. As a concession, though, she got off her bicycle and wheeled it up the densely tree-lined avenue. If I only had a camera, she thought and wondered why she had not thought of acquiring one back in London.

And then, to her surprise, as she turned the sharp corner at the top of the driveway and saw the small château featured in her postcard, she nearly bumped into a man with a camera on a tripod taking photographs.

'Oh, I say, would you mind awfully?' he asked.

'You're English!' she exclaimed in surprise.

'I certainly am!'

'What are you doing here?' she asked.

'I could ask you the same thing. Looks like we are both trespassing. But at least I have a good excuse ...'

'Taking photographs?'

He nodded. 'And you, Miss ...'

'I'm here on holiday. Looking at châteaux. Only most of them seem to be locked up or hidden away. This is the first one I have actually seen and I haven't seen it yet. It looks very closed up ...' She scrutinized the Château Remeillant and, in spite of herself, had to admit it was a bit disappointing. It was more of a big house really, with a turret at each corner, and wouldn't be too out of place in her stepmother's old copy of *Country Life*. Of course, it was more French than English. There was no water but a lot of weeds in the rather shallow moat. The turrets all had coned roofs covered with diagonally placed slates; one had a zinc weathervane topped by a copper cockerel set on its peak, drooping now at rather a jaunty angle. All the windows had closed shutters with peeling paint.

'The family went away at the start of the war and haven't come back. To all intents and purposes they have abandoned the place, but that's not to say they welcome visitors. There are so many threatening signs that when I heard your squeaky bike, I assumed it was one of the locals come to shoot me.'

'Well, no.' Laura smiled. 'But you don't seem too worried. About the locals coming to shoot you, I mean.'

'One of the hazards of my job.' The man turned back to his camera on its tripod. 'Well now you are here, I may as well use you.'

'Um ...'

'If you wouldn't mind putting that contraption down and then if you can go and stand looking up admiringly at the turret ... No over there,' he pointed impatiently. 'If you turn sideways on to me—chin up, no, not so much—yes, that's about right, raise your head—a bit more—and gaze in awe ... stay just like that! Don't move.'

She stayed just like that. She tried not to move.

She heard him laugh. 'That should do,' he said, and then remembered himself. 'Thanks awfully.'

'Your job is photographing châteaux? For a book?' Laura asked.

'A postcard company, actually. Frightful bore. Wouldn't mind if I never saw another of these so-called *chateauses* again! As long as I live. But,' he sighed, 'it's money in the pocket and I am nearly done. Back to Blighty tomorrow with my rolls of film. Seen hundreds of the blessed things in the last couple of weeks. Wish I had had you with me, though—photographs are so much better with people in them. Gives a sense of scale, if you know what I mean.'

'Oh, yes,' Laura said obligingly although she had no idea what he meant and, in any case, wouldn't it be rather odd, hundreds of postcards of châteaux all with the same girl in them! 'I borrowed a bicycle,' she tried to explain her own situation but the man wasn't interested. He was writing in his own notebook, one very like hers, only full of tiny handwriting.

'Have to keep a record,' he said cheerily. 'One notebook for my expenses and another for notes on the châteaux, don't want to muddle the confounded things up, can you imagine what Vernon Hicks would say?'

'Vernon Hicks?'

'Based in Bradford. Mr Vernon is known locally as Mr Postcard but in reality it's his late partner's widow, Mrs Hicks, who runs things. It's she who keeps a tight check on everything. Especially my expenses notebook. Have to record every last *centime*, if I don't want to be out of pocket. Which I don't.' He paused and looked sideways at Laura for a moment. 'Where are you staying?'

'Oh, at the Grand Hôtel du Bœuf ...'

'Very nice too!' he said sarcastically. "Fraid Vernon Hicks don't run to anything more than a roadside *auberge*. Shared rooms at that. Mrs Hicks is very strict.' He was chatting as he dismantled his apparatus and folded down the tripod. 'You can have no idea, unless you have stayed in one of those places, how loudly French commercial travellers snore. It's all the red wine they put away, I suppose. I only hope I haven't picked up any lice like I did last year snapping castles on the Rhine. Could have done with you there too.'

'But weren't there people at the castles you could have asked?' Laura said. He had dropped the posh English accent, she noticed. He was now a jobbing snapper. Under the thumb of Mrs Vernon Hicks in faraway Bradford.

'Yes, plenty! That was the problem on the Rhine. Hefty *Mädchens* in hideous great dirndl skirts kept pushing into the picture. I had to go back to a few of them *schlosses* and redo the postcards they wrecked.' He sighed bitterly. 'At my own expense.'

'Oh! I hope you don't decide later that I wrecked your picture here—of the Château Remeillant ...' As she gazed up again at the château, she thought she saw a shutter opening but on closer inspection it hadn't been fastened back correctly and was merely swinging in the breeze.

'I hope not too—that would prove an expensive error.'

'Can you, maybe, give me some tips?' Laura asked tentatively. 'Aren't there any nice châteaux—in cycling distance, that is—that are open to the public? I would so like to go inside one.'

The man laughed. 'You'd be lucky. You got caught by the guidebook too. I reckon it was written by the owner of that Grand Hôtel of yours wanting to get the punters in. It's true there is a high density of small châteaux in these parts—like what he says—but none you'll get to nosy around unless you have an "in" with the local grandees. Which you obviously haven't, so if I were you, I would just go and sit in the hotel gardens and enjoy the sun and think pretty thoughts. Or better still pack your bags and head for Paris. You look like a girl that gets easily bored.'

Laura smiled thinly and thanked the man for his advice as politely as she could, wished him luck with his photographs—for that seemed the thing to do—and then she wheeled the heavy bicycle about, climbed on it unsteadily and, concentrating hard on avoiding potholes, endeavoured to find the route back to the hotel.

For the next five days she cycled round the country lanes stopping for coffees (horrid little bitter coffees) and *pâtisseries* (sugary disappointing confections), no longer even attempting to locate the local châteaux. On the Friday she returned the bicycle to the porter, concierge or whatever he was, Philippe, who slipped her ridiculously large bank note quickly into his pocket without acknowledging it except to say that he would hand it on to his son, the proprietor of the *bicyclette*. He then tried to ask if she and her mother and sister had enjoyed their stay—she assured him that they all had, very very much!—but Philippe had then said something more pressing which she had not understood.

Dinner that evening was their last and she would be glad to get home to Paddington even though all those months she had spent anticipating this holiday would leave a void. What would there be now to look forward to? Laura smiled bravely. She would find something. Maybe a trip to those castles on the Rhine!

Isabel walked unaided into the dining room. 'You see,' she said brightly to Mr Hutton, installed as always at their table, 'my ankle is quite mended.'

Eleanor squeezed Laura's hand. 'I think Isabel has something to tell you,' she said.

The oddest thing about it all was that Mr and Mrs Hutton returned to the Grand Hôtel du Bœuf a year later. France had by then sufficiently recovered after the war to have mended a few of its potholes and to have a far greater abundance of postcards on offer for tourists to purchase.

'Poor Laura,' the couple laughed together at the sight of so many châteaux on the brand new rack of brand new cards available at the hotel kiosk. 'We never quite got to the bottom of it. Her obsession with the things.'

'She said she lost her notebook, do you remember, the one she stuck all her postcards in?

It tipped out of the bicycle basket into a ditch,' Godfrey reminisced.

'That's my sister for you!' Isabel reached out and picked a card from the rack. 'How ridiculous,' she said when she flipped it over, 'they're manufactured in Bradford, England. By a company called Vernon Hicks. You would have thought the French would want to make their own postcards.'

Godfrey Hutton snorted. 'Well, they are for the English tourists. I doubt if the French themselves bother much with ruins ...'

'Yes, but look, Godfrey dear—don't you think this girl looks awfully like Laura?'

'What's that?' Mr Hutton squinted at the picture his young wife was holding out to him. He eyed the figure in the picture. 'Could be anyone,' he said.

'I'd recognize Laura's stubborn chin and snub nose anywhere.' Again she turned the card over: '*Château Remeillant*. It's her, isn't it?'

Mr Hutton considered the card again. 'If you say so, my dear.'

Because the strangest thing had happened after they had made their happy announcement that evening at dinner. Laura had appeared next morning with her bag packed and said she was going to Paris.

'On your own?' Eleanor queried. 'Are you sure?'

'On your own!' Isabel was aghast. 'You can't.'

'On my own,' Laura said firmly. Her friend Philippe—Monsieur Denzat to the rest of them—had then driven her to the station so that she could catch the next train. And that was the last they had seen of her, until this postcard. She had sent a note with her congratulatory wishes and a little present for the wedding, and she had given an address in Montmartre so that, as she said, they could keep in touch but when the Huttons had called there on their way through Paris a few weeks ago, finding the correct street and then the right door, a pleasant woman draped in small children had answered their ring and informed them that Mademoiselle Laura had given up her room many months ago and travelled south. 'She has gone to learn to paint.'

'Paint!' Isabel was aghast.

'But she will be back. She will send an address. She promised. If you would care to leave me a note, I will give it to her when I can.'

'How stupid!' Isabel had exclaimed furiously. Trust Laura to disappear 'south' in order to 'learn to paint'. And after they had come all this way, panting up the steep streets of Montmartre specially. Who did she think she was? Van Gogh? Cezanne?

The woman with a baby at her breast and at least three small children clinging to her skirts (it was hard to count them) had blinked at her. '*Au contraire*,' she had said mildly but firmly. '*La*

Mademoiselle Laura n'est pas imbecile. Pas du tout! She eez not stupid. No, indeed.' She had reached over her baby's head and shut the door in their faces.

'I think I said the wrong thing,' Isabel murmured and Godfrey tucked her arm under his.

'Don't worry about it, my dear. Laura will reappear when she's ready.' He was of the firm and unshakeable opinion that the girl had envied her sister her good fortune in marrying his good self and had gone off in a jealous huff. Mary had also had a sister, Joyce, who had also envied Mary her good fortune in marrying Godfrey Hutton. Spent years doing so in fact.

'Yes, but Godfrey dearest. Laura, painting! It's absurd.'

THE WOOD ENGRAVER

YOU HAVE ASKED ME TO WRITE A FEW WORDS about my late friend, her *bravura gravura* as I have always been pleased to call her delightful wood engraving work, her life, her education, her family upbringing, her travels, her inspiration. Goodness knows what else. A Foreword—or is it an Introduction? (I have never truly known the difference)—to attach to a little volume of her pictures, beautifully printed on fine white rag paper, that you have been planning to offer to the art loving public. You first asked me to do this a year ago and I agreed, and when I met you last week, you reminded me of my promise. As if I had forgotten!!

The selection of her images is ready. The paper is folded and cut. The printers await. Three pages you said, just enough to paint a picture. Satisfy curiosity. Provoke interest. 'You know the kind of thing.'

I do indeed. Nevertheless, you present me with a considerable problem. What you ask for is not easy. Maybe it never is. What to say, and what to leave out. And in the case of my friend, Paulina, where on earth to start?

With the easy facts, perhaps. If they fill my three pages I will not be obliged to go on. To reveal those things that I think may be better to keep hidden. Her father was an illustrator. Had a long distinguished career—there was a time when everyone knew his work. If not his name. Those famous posters that were once splashed all over railway stations. Those rather comic caricatures that filled the weekly illustrated papers. Nowadays his artwork is 'dated' and of little interest. You rarely see it and when you do, derisory price labels are attached and invariably with inaccurate attributions and descriptions. I could give you lots of examples but his chocolate box paintings and engravings are not what is of interest here.

Paulina was his fifth and youngest daughter. By the time she was born to his third wife, he was already well embarked on the path that would eventually kill him. In short, he was drinking himself to death. She once told me that this was 'not all bad' because it meant she could quietly infiltrate his studio and squeeze out his oil paints and pick up his brushes and dab at his pictures in such a way that when he was sober again he assumed he himself had made the mess. Her other sisters and brothers took themselves away out of the home at the first opportunity that presented to them but she was happy to spend her young years haunting his studio, acting as a model when required, mixing his paints ...

He died leaving the family nothing. Less than. Everything he had was sold to settle his debts. At fifteen, Paulina had nothing in the world except ...

How gleefully she used to recount the true start of her own career!

Her father's last woman, Angelica—no room here to give chapter and verse since it is the daughter and not the father, or indeed this last woman I am writing about—had formed a close bond with poor Paulie, as she called her. They and they alone knew the truth.

Angelica said, don't be silly, Paulie. No need for tears. We are not impoverished. True we must leave this great house he constructed and was so fond of, and his purpose-built studio with all its pottery and textiles, but his debts must be paid and your brothers and sisters are hell bent on paying them. There is no reason you and I cannot continue together as if he was still alive.

As if Papa were still ...

By now the pair had removed to attic rooms owned by a rather outlandish but wealthy art collector friend of Paulina's father who had taken pity when he saw the auction vans arriving. The attics were unfurnished but adequate. The light was good. You can stay here until ...

Angelica arranged it all. Angelica was a very arranging sort of woman, which was just as well because she was not herself a lot older than Paulina, but she knew a great deal more about the ways of the world.

Before long, Angelica was of course living in the big rooms downstairs with the wealthy art collector friend of Paulina's late Papa. Paulina stayed happily in the attics and continued to produce her father's pictures, taking them to the newspaper and advertisement offices to sell, just as she had done in those last years when he was still alive but barely capable of working. 'Just tell them that your dear father left a lot of unpublished work you are authorized to sell ... ask them what they are looking for at the moment. Look as if you are trying to remember. Tell them you are pretty sure you have seen just the thing among your father's papers and will return in a day or so. Come straight home and get on with it. Without your father taking the money and spending it immediately in the public houses, you and I will soon be better off than we have ever been ...'

And so it proved. One thing led to another—as always happens when you recount the story of another's life. And ended with Angelica comfortably ensconced downstairs, eventually marrying the owner of the big house and when he died, owning it in its entirety, but choosing to share the place with the owner's disinherited son—an unpublished poet—who turned up at his father's funeral and with whom she then had three children.

Paulina went on living in the attic. Her desk was set under a window that somehow (a happy bubble in the ancient glass) magnified the light that came in. She had started wood engraving. She now issued these under her own name, although she changed her name to Paul. At first she told publishers that they were her brother's work. She made up endless stories. Paul was crippled and unable to leave the house. She bought him his inks and his woodblocks in Bleeding Heart Yard. It was quite amusing the stories she invented about this talented engraver, 'Paul'. Soon she let her father and his dated sentimental style die away. Her intricate engravings were much in demand. She was keenly sought after by the second rank of author who felt that fine illustrations might boost the popularity of their writing and hence their sales. No one paid a lot for them. No one was prepared in fact to pay any more for these intricately carved and printed engravings than they would have done for black and white drawings by any of the tens of thousands of jobbing artists who could turn out ink sketches to order. Paulina's painstaking illustrations had those lines and stippled shadows only engravings could produce. She worked long hours chipping away at her wood blocks up in that attic. Her siblings almost forgot about her existence. The small children in the house downstairs were always surprised when she came scurrying down through the house clutching folders of papers. A servant was detailed to attend on her and take her up food and keep her out of the way. This servant, a Miss Tite, treated poor Paulie with a mixture of contempt and fear. I suppose the truth is that she spent such long hours on her own in the attic, huddled over her work, she had become a trifle eccentric.

And this was the state of things for years. Until the advent into their lives of one Augustus Peartree. A bibliophile and museum curator. A man of great taste and discernment who had been invited to one of Angelica's popular artistic soirées. Unable to attend, he visited one morning to give his apologies in person and encountered Paulina on the stairs. He bumped into her so that she gave a little shriek, sending her papers scattering. Peartree did not look at her. He scarcely registered her presence as he started to amass the prints that had cascaded around his feet.

'Who did these?' He demanded, recognizing their style immediately as he shifted around on the floor picking them up. He did not hand them back. They were original Pauls, the ink scarcely dry!

Paulina gulped. 'Why, they are mine,' she admitted quietly. 'All mine. I have my studio in the attics here.'

The great man, standing upright now but still clutching her work, stared down at her. 'Here? In this house? Upstairs?'

She blinked, and nodded. 'You may come and see if you care to. I have an old hand press, an Albion dating from 1832—it's got a brass label, you see—but still going strong and ...'

And so began the one big friendship of her life. The two would meet at the British Museum. He bought her a camera. 'I am sending you abroad,' he said. 'I want you to travel and visit all the places you have been engraving all these years. See them for yourself. I will pay all your expenses. I want you to stay in the best hotels. Eat the best food. No expense spared. Why? Because I can no longer go myself. But you will write to me every week. Only once a week because you will have better things to do with your time than scribble missives to me. I shall expect you to tell me about everything of any interest that you see. Anyone you meet. You will make drawings. You will stay away for a year and a day. On your return, I will be on the platform at Victoria Station waiting for you. All I ask is that you describe all the sights to me in great detail. Do you agree?'

Paulina agreed.

It was her one great adventure. 'Only one?' you say. But it was a greater adventure than most people ever have. She sent her letters for a year and a day, as per the agreement, and then she did not return. There was no reunion at Victoria Station. Augustus Peartree was saved the bother of going there at some inconvenient hour and the expense of a platform ticket. Paulina had simply vanished. I was the only one who ever saw her again. My father sent me to find her. And I did. Tracking her down in Florence that long hot summer. So bright, so dazzling, so happy. But she forbade me ever to disclose the rest of her story. And luckily I have now over-run my three pages! You will have to guess the rest for yourself. Or simply accept that there are some things you will never be permitted to know. Just because you have the wherewithal to purchase this attractive volume of Paulina's *bravura gravura*—oh so beautifully printed on the finest white rag paper, no expense spared!—doesn't give you the right to pry into my dear friend's life.

Simeon Peartree D Phil, FRSA

A NEW POSTCARD RACK
CHASING CHÂTEAUX 2

'I HAVE BEEN THINKING, MY DEAR,' GODFREY Hutton began in his ponderous way while they were sitting on opposite sides of the tiny but cluttered dining table, waiting for the curious little *bonne bouche* plates to be removed (that can't have been compôte of snails, can it? Well, actually, yes, knowing the Grand Hôtel du Boeuf like they did, it probably can!). This evening, though, Godfrey had no interest in finding fault with the food. 'Yes, I have been thinking that it is high time you—or rather we, my dear—should have a word with your stepmother.'

'A word?' Isabel glanced at her husband sharply. 'With Eleanor?'

'When we get back.'

'Why? I mean, what about?'

'The flat.'

'In Paddington?'

Godfrey nodded. 'I think we should get on with it as soon as we return home.'

'So, you agree with me,' Isabel said with a bright smile. She had thought the place rather badly in need of a good clean and a thorough tidy up on her last visit the evening before they left for the Continent when she and Godfrey had gone to tell Eleanor that they would be out of the country for a few weeks. She was surprised her husband had noticed the state of the place. He had sat solidly in his chair throughout the visit, refusing a sherry. So why suddenly mention it now, all these weeks on? Weeks in which they had moved from hotel to hotel, finally arriving back here at the Grand Hôtel where a year ago, almost to the day, they had first met. She wasn't sure why they had to return to this horrible place. It wasn't as if it had been that nice the first time, except that of course it was here in these drab surroundings that they had encountered one another and, after she hurt her ankle, become engaged. Perhaps it had been in some way romantic, or sentimental, to have returned. 'You surely haven't been thinking about the state of the flat for the last three weeks have you, darling?' Isabel teased him.

'What's that?'

'All the time we have been touring?'

'No, but since we are about to head home ...'

'Are we? You didn't say.'

'Holidays can't go on forever,' Godfrey sighed. 'Much as we might like them to.'

'Well, yes, I think you are right. I am ready to go back to London. And really, I ought to have set about finding her someone who does.'

Mr Hutton's lips twitched. 'Who "does" what?' he asked irritably.

'I have a horrible feeling poor Eleanor has given up caring. She doesn't seem to notice the dust, or mind it very much. It often happens, I suppose, to people who live so entirely on their own. I doubt if she has seen anyone at all since we left. She probably hasn't even noticed.'

Mr Hutton stared at his wife. Wasn't it bad enough dealing with people speaking French every day and the natives so wilfully failing to understand everything he said, however loudly and clearly he made his demands clear. He was firmly of the opinion that anyone with the smallest ounce of intelligence can understand English perfectly well *if they try*. And now, here was Isabel deliberately not comprehending what he was trying to tell her. It had not been like this with Mary. Far from it! Poor Mary, god rest her soul, had usually known what he was going to say even before he opened his mouth. Odd, he reflected, how it had irritated him so much at the time when she had leapt in and answered his questions and comments before he had even had a chance to utter them! But then, especially towards the end, Mary had been a very irritating woman.

Isabel laughed, embarrassed at having casually used a common phrase she had picked up along the way. 'I mean a cleaning lady, of course. A woman who *does* the cleaning! If we had had time I would have popped in ...'

'Popped in!'

'Called, if you like, on Mrs Forster, on the floor below. Number fifteen. She's been there for years and I am sure she could recommend someone honest and hard-working if I asked her. And if not, she could certainly ask around for me. It would be by far the easiest way of coming up with ... Yes, I will go and see Mrs Forster as soon as we get back.' She did not mention Barry Forster, the boy she had been keen on at one time. But it would be nice if the Forsters, mother, son, and Barry's young bride, were to see how well she had done for herself, marrying Godfrey Hutton.

'That was not what I meant,' Mr Hutton said steadily. But he was interrupted by the arrival of the entrées. Two plates of ... seafood of some description swimming in the usual strange garlic sauce. They both stared at their plates. He thought perhaps next year they might holiday at home for a change. Brighton, Worthing, Hove, Southwold, Whitstable. Eastbourne, even. He had had enough of foreign.

'Good thing Laura isn't here,' Isabel laughed, raising her fork and plunging it into the pungent mess. She stirred it around a bit. A spoon would be more use. Laura who had always been very firm about not eating anything that had once lived and breathed—even if it was only in the sea, which was ridiculous in France. 'I wonder if she is still trying to be vegetarian.'

Godfrey Hutton had no intention of discussing the errant younger sister. Or her ridiculous eating habits. Or anything else about her. The longer the girl remained errant the better for all concerned was his decided opinion. Mr and Mrs Hutton ate for a while in silence. Then, after these plates had also, in their turn, been cleared and while they waited for a cheese and sweet course to be offered, he resumed his topic.

'Your stepmother really ought to make plans.'

'Plans, Godfrey? I don't think Eleanor ...'

It had been odd how when they had first met, here in this shabby hotel, Isabel had wondered fleetingly if Eleanor and Mr Hutton might not come to some arrangement. She had mentioned it to Laura who immediately said it was impossible for their father to be so swiftly replaced. Or ever replaced. And so it had been she ...

'About the apartment,' Godfrey impatiently interrupted her thoughts. Was the girl really so obtuse? 'It is obviously far too big for her on her own. You saw the state of the place. She never even goes into half the rooms. And since you and Laura each own a share ...'

'Laura and I share it, yes. Well, we *will* share it when Eleanor goes. But that's obviously not for a long time yet—so there is nothing really to discuss.'

'I wouldn't say that, Isabel, my dear. The fact is, I think there is a great deal to discuss. A great deal indeed. '

'Oh?' Isabel had no idea what he could mean.

'The place should be sold and the proceeds shared three ways. I will help you invest yours and then in due course, you will no doubt inherit your half of your stepmother's collateral and I will help you invest that too.'

'Goodness, Godfrey, that is all very mathematical! But doesn't it add up to the very same thing? I will get half eventually, either way.'

'In the long run, maybe, but in the short term, no—it's not the same thing at all. In the short term, you would get most of what was coming to you now. But since it comes to you from your father who is deceased, it is only right you should have the benefit.'

'But I don't need any "benefit", as you call it. And Eleanor wouldn't want the bother of selling up and moving. I wouldn't want her to. I like the fact that the flat is still there as it always was. My childhood home. I can go back in time whenever I please.' Isabel chose profiteroles and Godfrey waved the *carte* away. They had been foolish to return here when they knew the food was so indifferent.

Isabel sliced the gooey confection before her in silence. Was Godfrey Hutton in fact a brides-in-the-bath murderer? What did they know of him? Really and truly. Except that he had been married to a "Mary" who had died about the same time as father. But had she died? What if Godfrey had bumped her off? And would he now bump her off simply for her half share of the dingy Paddington mansion flat? She wished Laura were here to laugh about it with her. Or would Laura laugh? Might in fact there be some truth. Certainly Mr Hutton—Godfrey—was not laughing.

'Don't we already have enough money?' Isabel asked lightly. 'I thought you had sold your business very profitably?' He had owned some factory in the North of England that had been in the Hutton family for years. It had been bought out by a partner, or something like that. There had been some bother over the transaction but Godfrey had not been very clear on the matter.

'You can never have enough money, my dear,' Godfrey replied grimly. 'And you never know what may be just around the corner ...' His greatest fear, he explained, was that Eleanor would remarry and the ownership of the flat would slip away. He had not voiced this fear yet but he foresaw there would come a time when he might have to.

'Ah, well, yes.' Isabel smiled. If silly Laura had not become so ridiculously keen on visiting châteaux, we would never have come here. And we—Godfrey and I—might never have met. Her husband was right—you never knew what was round the corner.

'You know,' Isabel said, 'I wonder if Laura was actually on to something.'

'Your sister!'

'Yes. I want to go and see a château or two for myself. There's nothing else at all to do round here. I can't imagine how we ended up here the first time, let alone coming back here now. Let's hire a car.'

'Hire a ...'

'We can ask the porter, the obliging Monsieur Denzat. Laura's Philippe!'

'Strictly speaking, the fellow is a concierge ...'

'Whatever he is! He behaves as if he owns the place. I want you to go and ask about a car!' It was the first time Isabel had snapped at her husband.

Godfrey Hutton blinked and placed his hand with melodramatic sorrow over hers. 'My poor dear!' he exclaimed sorrowfully. 'I see you have already tired of my company. You are bored.'

'No, Godfrey,' Isabel replied obstinately. She was not to be deflected. 'I just want to ... I can't see any reason why I should not go and see the Château Remeillant for myself.'

'If that is what you want ...'

'It is!'

Godfrey duly went to enquire about a car. While he tapped his room key impatiently on Monsieur Denzat's desk as telephone calls were made—there had been no telephone at the hotel on their last visit, he was certain about that— Mr Hutton had time to reflect on his wife's unprecedented display of temper. He smiled to himself. It could only mean one thing. A little

Hutton on the way at last. He would say nothing but the moment they got back to Blighty he would have a word with Biffy at the club. Get the boy—assuming it was a boy—on the waiting list at the school. Steal a march on the other unborn fellows, hadn't that always been his way? Wouldn't that be the way, too, of his son. For of course it would be a boy. Hadn't Godfrey read somewhere that the sex of a baby depended on the vigour of a man's thrust and Godfrey Hutton certainly knew how to thrust vigorously! Hadn't he proved that over the last year with his new young wife. He heard himself humming a happy tune.

He tipped Monsieur Denzat an absurdly generous amount. 'That'll put a few chickens in the pot,' he chuckled. *'Ca va mettre quelque poulets dans la marmite!'* He had memorized the phrase from a section of Useful Phrases for the Traveller in the back of a guidebook Mary had once bought.

'Bien sûr, Monsieur Hutton. We, at the Grand Hôtel du Boeuf, like veree much to geev satisfaction.'

The car was arranged for the following morning. A signature and excessively large deposit were required. 'And the other one?' the concierge enquired when the paperwork was completed.

'Eh?'

'Mademoiselle Laura?'

'I don't know anything, old chap,' Hutton replied with a shrug of his shoulders and then, safe in the knowledge that he would not be understood, he added, 'except that she is about to become an aunt.'

'An ant? *Un formi?*' Philippe Denzat shook his head.

The car, when it swept up the tree-lined drive the following morning, was driven by a young man wearing spotless white gloves who politely introduced himself as Florian. 'I am your chauffeur for the day,' he said bowing low. 'I am here to take you wherever you please. But I understand it is your wish to visit the Château Remeillant.'

'Oh, yes, please!' Isabel answered. If only Laura were here to see the ease with which she herself had arranged things. No renting some soldier's dangerous *bicyclette* for her!

'My, his English is very good,' Godfrey Hutton observed. 'Not like the rest of them ...'

Life was most satisfactory, he reflected as he sank back into his seat behind Florian who eased the car down the drive, past the very spot where Isabel had come a cropper last year (you could even see a slight dent in the solid trunk of the chestnut tree if you looked carefully) and then turned on to the public road heading in the direction of the Château Remeillant.

Isabel, sitting up beside the chauffeur in the front, stared straight ahead and thought, Laura must have come this way on that heavy old bicycle. Bumping over the potholes left by German lorries and tanks.

When they arrived at the Château Remeillant they were taken aback to find the gates open, the shutters and windows were also open. An elderly lady and some tall thin dogs came down the front steps to greet them.

'This is my family home,' said Florian, kissing his mother on both cheeks. 'Pray enter, do.'

SUMMER HOLIDAY

KATHLEEN AND WIN HAD VERY LITTLE IN COMMON, meeting as they had done—and indeed, did do every day during term time—in the 'staff common room' of St Elda's, the girls' school where they had both found themselves teaching. Neither had actually had any particular ambition to become a teacher. It had 'just happened' to both of them. Perhaps this was why they sought each other's company. For they were both disconcerted by the undisguised enthusiasm and dedication the other occupants of the 'common room' displayed for their posts as teachers. They were both, in truth, a little outraged by it all. This large fusty room, with old carpets and worn leather chairs, and the endless little competitions. Worst of all was Miss Burnon (whom they both secretly, to one another, called The Bunion) with her assiduous rotas and schemes.

'Your turn this week,' she told Win, shaking the kettle with typical Bunion gusto. 'Tea and coffee duty! Make sure everyone—without excebption—puts their twopence in the tin!' Win winced. Kathleen giggled often drank multiple cups of coffee without contributing to the tin. It was her biggest rebellion. That, and the pottery master ...

There had been a man—yes, a man!—teaching pottery one year. He had not lasted the year. Miss Vickers, the headmistress, had had to have a very unfortunate interview with the fellow after parents had complained. He had been dispatched so swiftly it was as if he had never been. Not that he had ever joined colleagues in the 'common room'. It had been the year Kathleen came to the school. She remembered him clearly enough because her heart had missed the odd beat but she had known she was not the only one. They had shared a cup of coffee. Out of a pottery mug. But it turned out there had been a lot of coffee shared that year in the little kitchen in the art block where she had taken refuge that never-to-be-forgotten but never-to-be-remembered afternoon. Ten years back.

Win's arrival at the school to teach the younger girls French had been a relief. She had been someone to sit with, and chat to, about things that weren't tedious amendments to the school rules or new regulatory requirements regarding the dowdy uniform the girls were obliged to wear. 'The uniform must be rigorously enforced in every tiny detail,' Miss Vickers liked to repeat at every opportunity. They were 'Miss Harkness' and 'Miss Vale' even to each other. It was only now, that Kathleen Harkness and Winifred Vale agreed that they would be Kath and Win over the summer. They were on holiday!

Standing on deck on the ferry to Ostend, trying to fend off the awful possibility of being seasick, a sharp wind whipping their faces, Kath and Win felt they had at last escaped. When they had met up at Victoria station in London, Kathleen had scrutinized Win's cardboard suitcase and her plastic hold-all and demurred for a moment at the suitability of Win as a companion on this particular journey that had come to symbolize more—so very much more!—than a six week stay in a little town in the middle of France that Win had somehow known about. 'I will make all the arrangements,' Win had said. It had sounded so wonderful to have a proper summer holiday at last, but there was nothing wonderful about the suitcase, the hold-all or indeed Win's bright orange plastic mac. Kathleen could not know that Win had similar misgivings. Kathleen was too impractical. It was cold and wet, and look at her! Not even a mackintosh. Win couldn't now remember why when she had told Kath that she intended going over to France for the summer and Kath had murmured something like: 'Oh, how wonderful! Lucky you!' she had then felt impelled to say; 'Come with me if you like.' It wasn't as if they were truly friends. Just acquaintances who suffered together in that frightfully stuffy school common room.

Kathleen stared at the grey sea and thought of Kenneth. Imagine perishing in that! But what chaos he had left behind.

'What about Angela?' Kathleen had asked.

'Bit late worrying now,' Kenneth said. The girl should have said 'no' last night, and he would have left well alone. Angela, his fiancé, had been out when he called. Better Kathleen than no one on his last evening, he had decided, inviting the young skinny sister to accompany him to the pub and the pictures. They had not got to the pictures.

'I've hardly seen her this leave, Kenneth grumbled. 'I even wonder if she's got someone else.'

Kathleen drew her legs up to her knees, hiding her nakedness rather shyly. 'Ange works long hours at the munitions. They don't get time off.'

'I'll sort it all when I'm back,' Ken said, pulling her to him again. 'When this blasted war is over.'

By the time news came that his ship had gone down, Ange was several months pregnant. There had been a showdown at home. Kathleen watched. Her father furious, her mother tight-lipped. The shame, the disgrace, they repeated. Then Ange announced that the baby wasn't Kenneth's, but his brother's. 'When Malcolm comes home we are going to get married. He wanted to square it

96

with Ken before he left, but didn't get a chance.' Malcolm was now somewhere in the Far East. A Japanese prisoner-of-war camp. It didn't bear thinking about.

'Well, I hope for your sake he does come back,' their father said wearily.

Malcolm had returned and he and Ange had married and a couple of months later Malcolm had put a service revolver he had somehow managed to retain into his mouth and shot himself. Ange and her two babies lived at home with Mum and Dad. Kathleen went off to teach at St Elda's, a friend of hers having vacated the job to marry. 'The place is stuck in the country, miles from anywhere, but you'll be all right,' the friend said breezily. 'The girls aren't the brightest and most of the staff are as thick as two short planks ... you'll like the art teachers though. They come and go, and the other teachers can't stand them, Miss Bunion in particular, but at least they are alive. More or less.' She herself was marrying a friend of her brother's who had lost an eye at Dunkirk.

'Penny for them,' Win said, hanging on tight to the railing.

'Oh, I'm sorry,' Kath shook herself. 'All that water makes me feel ... I was thinking about Dunkirk. For some reason.'

'I'm a bit queasy myself,' Win said to show she wasn't fooled. 'But look—we are coming in now ... best get the luggage together. *Nous devons trouver nos bagages ...*'

Well, of course, Win spoke French. She taught it, didn't she? But Win speaking French was so unlike the usual Win ... Kath, who had done French at school but not used it since, wasn't sure she was going to enjoy depending on her companion. 'I have forgotten most of my French,' she confessed.

'You'll pick it up again,' Win said.

Kath shrugged.

They boarded the train bound for Paris. A surly porter had tried to take their cases off them but Win had firmly refused his offer of help. 'Five francs each! You have to be joking. *Vous plaisantez*!' Win laughed in his face. 'Trying it on because we are *anglaises*!' she told Kath.

Kath felt out of her depth. She would have been happy to pay for some help with her case. When the train had barely started up and with much squeaking and lurching was chugging along towards Paris, Win struck up a conversation—in French—with the lady whose carriage they had entered.

After a while the conversation lapsed and Kath said, slightly huffily—annoyed at having been so entirely left out—'what was that all about then?'

'Nothing much.' Win went into her hold-all to pull out some knitting. Hideous chunky knitting. Kath stared out through the grimy train windows at the darkening skies.

In Paris, Win bustled them onto a bus outside the *Gare du Nord* that trundled across the city to another station where they caught another train. All Kath had to do was follow in her wake.

'It's good you've found yourself a friend at that place,' her mother had said when Kath explained about the holiday.

Win wasn't exactly a friend. 'She's nice enough, I suppose. I am sure I will have a nice time.'

'I hope so, dear. You certainly deserve a holiday,' her mother had said.

I've been at that awful school ten whole years now, Kath thought. I shouldn't still be thinking about Ken. Ange doesn't. Ange didn't even think about Malcolm who had blown his brains out. She had remarried. A pleasant solid policeman who had his own house. There were three more babies. Not that they, or even the solid policeman, made Ange happy. She grumbled and complained all the time. She poked fun at the policeman, who was too goodhearted to notice.

It was ten o'clock at night, and dark, when the train pulled into the station Win had been looking out for. She and Kath struggled down onto the long-deserted platform, heaving their luggage with them. The train barely waited for them to do so before pulling away again and leaving them alone, in the dark and quiet in what felt like the middle of nowhere.

'I thought you said you had organized a taxi,' Kath said. She tried not to show her exasperation.

'It'll come.' Win picked up her things and began heading along the long dark platform towards a shelter they could see in the far distance. Kath had no choice but to follow and was startled when a man emerged from the bushes beside them. Win scarcely acknowledged his presence, but she let him take her cardboard suitcase. He made as if to take Kath's case from her, but she shook her head and indicated she preferred to carry it herself. Win took no notice and was already marching ahead as if leading the way. Kath felt a new surge of annoyance. Win clearly knew what she was doing but hadn't thought to explain anything of her arrangements to her travelling companion. Kath began to think that perhaps she might take herself off in the morning. Find a quiet hotel on her own to eke out the holiday. Before she knew it, though, she was in the back of an old car being driven somewhere by the man. Win was sitting in front, chattering nineteen to the dozen in French. Kath tried to look out of the window but could see nothing beyond shadowy fences, hedges, odd road signs and heavy trees looming on either side of the road when briefly lit by the car's headlights. I could be anywhere in the whole wide world, she thought, for all anyone knows or cares.

Kath must have dozed off because she awoke when the car stopped and Win called back to her, 'Here we are, Kath!'

Kath reached for the door handle and began clambering out of the back seat of the car, pulling her luggage with her. The driver attempted to take it from her, but again she held onto it. She saw his face for the first time. It had an enormous scar down one side. Win, still wearing her orange mac and her hair clips, led the way up a grand flight of steps to enormous heavy doors that appeared to swing open of their own accord. Kath imagined this was some inordinately expensive hotel and found herself vaguely regretting that she had not discussed their budget for daily expenses more carefully in advance. She probably doesn't care how much it costs, since I am paying half, she thought grudgingly.

Kath followed Win into the grandest foyer of a hotel she had ever seen. It was full of people. A loud cheer went up. A man with an extravagant medal hanging from an extravagant red, white and blue ribbon stepped forward and made a speech in French accompanied by more cheering and clapping. Win was now in the centre of the group of people, holding an enormous bouquet of flowers. The speech ended with a line of bad English. 'Eeet is our pleasure to have you back again with us, Mademoiselle Winifred. And your friend. For the summer. This will always be your second home. You will always be our guest of honour.' The clapping was long and loud. Kath found a glass of something fizzy pressed into her hand.

'Best not ask anything,' Win said later that night as they were preparing for bed. 'I was here in the war helping people get over the river into free France.'

'People?'

'Airmen, Jews fleeing deportation, escaped prisoners ...'

'You never said.'

'I promised one day I would come back. I wasn't sure if they would be pleased to see me. The world moves on. Those were difficult times for them.'

'Why didn't you tell me? When we planned the holiday together.'

'I have told no one. I am not telling you now. Just accept and enjoy this beautiful place. Ask no questions. What happened, happened. I lived when others didn't. That is why we are here. Now we must get some sleep or we will be good for nothing in the morning.'

Kath slept well. She awoke to find herself in the prettiest bedroom she had ever seen. Delicate gilded furniture. A washstand with real violet soap, soft fluffy towels and flannels draped over the side. She washed and dressed and ventured out. The house was quiet. She went gingerly down an enormous wooden staircase to find breakfast laid out at a big dining table. Bowls of fresh fruits, jars of *compôte* and *confiture*, fresh croissants and pastries were piled high together with a choice of different loaves of bread. The china was white, fine and sparkling and with a gold monogram painted on every piece. The cutlery ivory handled and silver.

A maid entered the room and when Kath said 'toilet' and then 'wc', she was ushered to a small room behind the staircase. On returning she found Win seated at the table.

'There you are, Kath,' she said. 'I thought I'd let you sleep in. Sit down, sit down. I'm famished. Oh, what a feast!'

Kath did as she was told.

Kath spent the rest of the holiday doing as she was told. She did not have much choice, not having enough French to make her presence felt. It was Win's holiday. These were Win's friends. The woman she had disregarded at the school except as someone to have a cup of tea and a moan with, was obviously held in high esteem. The pair of them took part in so many gatherings and celebrations, all of which involved eating copiously and sampling wines and other drinks made by their hosts. Who owned the mansion—or château, as Win called it—Kath never discovered. It was certainly not an hotel.

And then there was Sebastien.

On their last evening, Sebastien appeared out of the darkness and crouched down beside her while she was sitting on her own watching the bonfire. Someone was singing, someone else playing a flute. She could not see the scar down his face for it was on the other side from her. 'I speak a little *anglais*,' he said. Kath nodded, wondering what was coming next. 'We will be sorry when you leave us. But before you go, I want to tell you something.'

'Oh?'

'If it wasn't for your friend, I wouldn't be alive. Many of us around this bonfire tonight wouldn't be here if it wasn't for her bravery. Probably none of the children. I suppose she is famous at home? You both work in a school? I imagine the pupils adore her.'

Kath did not know what to say. 'Well, of course, only natural ...'

'I was there the night the escape party was ambushed. If it wasn't for the courage and quick thinking of Mademoiselle Winifred Vale. She stood up to the Germans and made them stop firing. She worked a miracle that night. To us, she is a saint. But, now! The dancing starts. Come and have the first dance with me.'

Despite her protests that she didn't dance and hadn't danced for years, and frankly didn't want to dance with a man with a nasty scar, Kath found herself held tight around the waist and whisked round and round amidst the other revellers. Occasionally she caught sight of Win twirling dumpily near her. Win was not a natural dancer. The night turned into morning. The bonfire died down and the crowd had dwindled and those that were left made their way to the château where the two teachers were staying. Arrangements were made for the drive back to the station in the morning.

'I am tired,' Win said when they were alone at last and climbing the stairs to bed.

'Me too,' Kath agreed. She wanted to ask Win about Sebastien but she was not sure what it was precisely she wanted to ask. About the scar down his face, she supposed. Had someone tried to cut him in two?

'Better pack before you go to sleep,' Win said. 'We are leaving at first light.'

Kath undressed and climbed into her bed and as she drifted into sleep she thought about her decision. Almost immediately it seemed, Win was leaning into her room saying the car was waiting.

Sebastien drove them to the station and when the train came, packed already with passengers, he climbed aboard, finding them seats and storing their bags in the overhead shelf. By the time Kath had settled herself in her seat, the train was moving. He had gone.

'The end of the summer holidays,' Win said. 'Back to The Bunion's twopenny tin!' She smirked.

Kath thought, I need to tell her. I need to say that I will not be travelling further than Paris. The holiday that she had feared would cost her all her savings had turned out to be remarkably cheap. They had lived well and hardly had to pay for anything. She had sent her mother a postcard, but even then someone had given her both the card and the postage stamp. Most of the money she had brought with her was still in her purse in the little leather handbag resting on her lap. Kenneth had bought it to give Angela but then presented it to Kath that final morning. 'You may as well have this,' were his exact words. This holiday had been the first time she had used it. She would stay in Paris as long as she possibly could. Beyond that she did not know, but one thing was certain, she would not be returning to St Elda's.

And it was true.

Twenty minutes later the train crashed headlong at full pelt into one from Paris coming, also at full pelt, in the opposite direction. Someone in a junction box had pulled the wrong levers. Someone else meanwhile helped themself to the little leather handbag (miraculously still intact and complete with purse inside) they found thrown a long way down the embankment from the mangled wreckage making identification of its owner impossible. The cash was very welcome and felt like manna from heaven. The rest of the contents and the bag itself were swiftly disposed of. I know not how.

'I hope Kath wasn't involved,' her mother remarked when they heard about the railway disaster, the worst apparently in postwar France. She was then relieved to receive a postcard. "Had such a lovely time here, I've decided to decide to stay on. Indefinitely. Will write again, as and when. Love to you all, Kath."

Her mother raised her eyebrows. 'I am not altogether surprised,' she said, handing the card to her elder daughter who happened to be visiting.

'It'll be a holiday romance,' Ange laughed. 'And good for her! About time poor Kath had a bit of fun.'

GODFREY HUTTON DREAMS
CHASING CHÂTEAUX 3

THE CHEESE PLATTER WAS DEFINITELY HIS downfall. Hadn't dear Mary always warned him: 'Godfrey, not too much camembert! You know what it always means.' But Mary was not the one with him that evening at the Grand Hôtel du Boeuf, so Godfrey had let the waiter pile his plate high with slim slices of all the local *fromages*, including some deliciously creamy camembert, with the inevitable consequence: he was dreaming.

In his dream, Mary was offering him a scone. 'Take one,' she said aggressively. 'In fact, take two.' She held out a plate of scones that might have been stones picked up on a beach, so large and smoothed, as if by the sea, did they look. They were heavy too. You could do a lot of damage with a plate of scones like these.

'Oh no, I couldn't, my dear. I have only just had my dinner.'

Mary laughed. It was not a nice laugh. 'I know you have,' she said. 'You haven't changed one bit. You know how to pack it away and no mistake.'

Godfrey shrugged. He ate his way through the great scone she had banged down in front of him, leaving a nasty crack across his china plate. Then he started obediently on another. She was pouring him tea now out of an enormous teapot that had three spouts.

'So what's all this I hear? A baby at your age! You silly old man!'

'A son and heir,' Godfrey retorted, his mouth full of scone. There was a sultana stuck to one of his front teeth.

'I doubt it. Some spoilt girl, more like, who will give you a lot of grief in your dotage. It's what you deserve.'

'I see no call to be quite so unpleasant, Mary. Goodness knows, you had your chances.'

'Huhh!' Again that nasty laugh. 'At the Grand Hôtel du Boeuf! I doubt if any child was ever conceived in that dreadful dreary place. Why ever did you always insist on going back there? Why ever have you brought your new young bride here?'

'You used to say you liked the place. You used to insist we return every year.'

'Only because I hoped to meet that nice Frenchman again.'

'Don't mention him to me. You were never the same after ...'

'After what, Godfrey? Go on, Godfrey. What was I never the same after?'

'You know perfectly well.'

'Yes, of course I do. But I want you to tell me.'

'Leave it! You know what happened last time you goaded me like this.'

'Yes, I do. And weren't the police hopeless. The way they accepted your pathetic tale. As if a woman like me would fall head first down the stairs, just like that. But the police will get you eventually, Godfrey. You mark my words. They always do, in the end.'

Godfrey turned over in bed. He could hear Isabel gently snoring. He wondered when she would tell him about the baby. He would buy her a ring. That is what he would do. He would have a ring ready in his pocket. A pearl. 'A pearl for a pearl,' he would say and then give her a nice juicy kiss on the lips.

He drifted back into sleep. 'You perfect fool,' Mary scoffed. 'That girl will need more than a pearl ring and great slobbery kiss to keep her happy when she finds out about the man she married. You will have to keep snipping pieces out of old newspapers to make sure she never reads the full story ...' On and on she went, nagging away until the noisy dawn chorus outside the window took over the task tormenting Godfrey Hutton. 'It's an *aubade*,' Mary said. 'That's French for dawn chorus. There's something you can teach your young bride over breakfast. One word of advice, though, Godfrey. For old time's sake. Best leave the cheese trolley well alone in future. At your age—I was going to say "our" age, but of course *I* am not aging any more, you spared me that humiliation, at least—camembert plays havoc with the digestion. And wrecks any chance of a good night's sleep.'

Godfrey woke to bright light filling the room. He blinked and sat up to find Isabel fully dressed and the shutters and windows wide open letting the sunlight stream in. 'What time is it?' he asked.

'Nearly mid-day. I went downstairs and had my breakfast so as not to wake you. You were fast asleep. I rather think all this château visiting has tired you out.'

'You had breakfast downstairs without me?' Godfrey was astonished.

'I sat at our own little table all by myself,' Isabel said with a pleasant enough laugh.

THE RIGHT FACE

'You have used my face, sir,' said Herbert Leadbetter, spluttering with anger.

'A fine face, if I may say so. Well suited to the purpose. It took us a long time to source one suitable for the job.'

'The job?'

'For the author of *Love's Illusion*. We combed far and wide.'

'But you have used it without my permission. You had no business.'

'On the contrary, sir. It is our business. That is precisely what it is. But never fear, we will pay you amply. Backdated, of course, and with compound interest.'

Herbert Leadbetter stared at the man. Was he so out of touch? Had England changed to such an extent during his fifteen-year absence that this kind of conversation was considered normal now?

'Pay me?' he repeated incredulously. Surely this made no commercial sense. Or any sort of sense. And yet, as he himself would be the first to admit, Leadbetter possessed no commercial skills, he had shown himself lacking in whatever it was that enabled some men to turn their dreams and efforts into cash. He thought back to that dread morning a few months back when the apologetic bailiff had arrived, puffing up the remote hill, a man with whom he had shared a drink on a number of occasions at the club. He had been pleasant enough while going about his wretched task, even managing to convince Herbert that he was doing him a favour, removing the worry, drawing a line. When all the machinery and chattels were labelled, the man had shaken him by the hand, thanked him for his cooperation and predicted that one day he would remember this moment and be glad. 'I've seen it time and again, sir,' he said as he climbed back on his horse. 'My advice to you is to go back to England, put this behind you, start anew.'

'Grow what?' Margaret had demanded. She always said coffee was a mistake. Everyone knew it was tea that grew best in Ceylon. After fifteen years she had been proved right. They had had to sell his father's gold watch to pay for their passages home.

'Indeed,' Mr Preinter said. 'We will pay you well.'

'For what, exactly?' Herbert pulled out a chair and sat down. Preinter, whose office it was, sat down too.

'For the use of your face, of course.'

'This is absurd. You have stolen ...'

'We have taken nothing from you.'

'But there are people out there who believe ...'

Herbert felt feverish. He leant over the desk and picked up a copy of the offending article. *Love's Illusion!* He turned it over and contemplated the picture of himself—undeniably of himself—printed on the back. 'People will look at that photograph and see my name and believe I wrote this book. It is an absurd situation. You are obviously the individual responsible.'

Preinter cupped his hands and rested them complacently on his desk. 'I can indeed claim that honour.'

'Honour? It is an outrage.'

'How so? The volume is in its eleventh impression. We have ordered a twelfth. *Love's Illusion* has become a sensation. A *succès fou* as we say in the profession.'

'Profession! What kind of profession is it that can turn a law-abiding citizen like myself, without his say-so, into a ...'

'Come now, sir, you are still a law-abiding citizen. You have not—certainly in so far as this matter is concerned—broken any laws.'

'You have turned me into some kind of impostor. A man others believe to have written a damnable bestseller, eleven impressions of which have already, apparently, been let loose on the streets. It is a scandal.'

'Only if you make it into one.'

'I beg your pardon.'

'We at Preinter & Preinter's have no interest in this affair ever becoming known beyond these walls. Indeed, we are prepared to pay you a sizeable sum of money for it to remain a happy secret between ourselves.'

'You are going to pay me to ...'

'We will pay you to be Herbert Leadbetter.'

'I am Herbert Leadbetter!'

' ...author of this book.'

'But I have never written a word in my life. Apart from inventories and lists, the odd letter to the bank, a postcard or two to my mother years back when she was still alive ...'

'You won't need to write anything. The book as you can see for yourself is already written. Its author, conveniently, is known as a recluse.' Preinter picked up the copy of *Love's Illusion* and read from the biographical note beneath the photograph, which he himself had composed. "A retiring man wedded to his typewriter, who spends his days in a darkened book-lined study hidden away in the shires." All we ask of you, Mr Leadbetter, is that you stay in your book-lined study. We will pay you amply to do so.'

'You are forgetting something, sir.'

'What is that?'

'I am not wedded to my typewriter. I do not even possess a typewriter. I am, though, wedded. To a wife who will most certainly not like any of this. Margaret is a straightforward honest woman. She is in poor health. The tropics have not been kind to her. Her sister came out to live with us a few years ago after both their parents passed on, and herself died only recently, shortly before my coffee estate failed. It was touch and go whether poor Margaret would make it to Southampton. She is now in need of expensive medical treatment.'

'The arrangement between us will provide all the medical treatment your wife can require. She will assuredly be pleased.'

It was ages since anything had pleased Margaret. She would surely take a dim view. Her younger sister, though, would have giggled 'fit to burst' as she herself would have put it. Dear sweet Catherine would have insisted on going over the details of this encounter, laughing uproariously. 'A pince-nez? Mr Preinter of Preinter & Preinter's actually wears a pince-nez?' She had always delighted in anything absurd, which was why she had encouraged Mr McBeanie, their neighbour in Ceylon, when she had no intention of accepting him. No intention whatsoever.

With a jolt, Herbert recalled a very odd evening a few years back, when he had been at the club in the company of this same McBeanie. The man had introduced a photographer, a fellow

Scot, whom he said was passing through. At the time, Leadbetter had thought this was unusual. No one 'passed through' those parts. The visitor had bought him a drink and then insisted on taking his photograph. Late into the evening, McBeanie had told the man that Leadbetter lived in the hills with two sisters. There had been something spiteful about the way he had spoken. 'He keeps the pair of them for his own exclusive use,' were McBeanie's words. Could this affair constitute the disappointed McBeanie's revenge? Herbert eyed Preinter. 'How did you acquire my picture?' he asked.

Preinter replied readily. 'From one of those photographers who go round the world discovering likenesses to purvey for purposes such as these. We were told you lived several days' ride from the nearest town, and enjoyed unusual domestic arrangements which made it most unlikely you would return to England.'

Herbert shrugged. It was true he had not expected to return. He had not known that Catherine would die, or that his crop would fail. He stared at Preinter. 'It is all such a confounded cheek,' he said weakly.

Preinter smiled. 'Have you spoken of this to others? Have you taken your wife, or any other person, into your confidence?' 'No, indeed, when I found out about it I came straight here. We arrived at Southampton at first light yesterday and immediately took the train to

London. Our fellow passengers went to a hotel near the docks but we were anxious to see a physician who had been recommended to us. On the train, I noticed a man reading a book with a photograph on the back. He kept glancing at me and then at his book jacket, doing so with such frequency I became uncomfortable. My wife was luckily too languid to notice. By the time we reached London, I had determined to speak to the fellow, but just as we were getting off the train he thrust a pen into my hand and asked me to sign his book. I tried to decline, but my wife was fretting over the luggage so I took his pen and scribbled 'With best wishes from the author', thinking that the author would like as not wish the man well. He went off happily and I did not give the matter further thought until the evening when my wife having been consigned to a clinic, I was dining alone. This time, a young woman accosted me. She started talking with such enthusiasm of my work that I had no opportunity to put a halt to her attention. Indeed, she ended up dining with me.'

'Did you let on?'

'That was what was so awkward. Because I did not do so at once, it became impossible subsequently. It was only this morning, finding myself in Cornhill, I decided to ...' Herbert did not feel the need to explain how he had met the girl again that morning and that she had accompanied him on his walk. It was she who had drawn attention to Preinters.

'Oh, I say!' the girl had gasped. 'Preinter & Preinter's. Two doors along. Have you come to talk to them about your next book?'

'My next book?' Herbert faltered. 'Talk to who?'

'You can't hide anything from me,' she giggled. 'I have been trying to publish myself. Without any success. I once visited Preinter & Preinter's to deliver a manuscript. But they sent it back the next day. I do not think they read a single page. How I long to see my photograph on the back of a book. Perhaps you would be ever such a darling and put in a good word?'

He smiled encouragingly at her and she squeezed his arm affectionately. Then she halted beside a doorway and pointed up some stairs. 'They are on the second floor. If you get a chance to remind them of Charmian Rivers—that's the name I use. Tell them I shall be sending another novel shortly. Set in Paris. If you could persuade ...'

'I will do my best, my dear,' Herbert heard himself telling her. The girl fluttered her fingers at him as he turned and began to make his way up the stairs.

'What of the real author? Why could he not have his name and picture attached to the book?'

'Ah!' Preinter smiled. 'I'm afraid it doesn't work like that. Instead of relying on one particular writer to write as the fancy takes him, we at Preinter & Preinter's prefer to spread the effort and control the outcome. Books are a crop—like your coffee—which we harvest as and when we please. We pay you to be the author and we employ others to do the work. It is a common enough arrangement and quite satisfactory.'

'I never heard of such a thing,' Herbert muttered.

'You only have to look at the number of books which authors like Charles Dickens and Anthony Trollope are supposed to have produced. Ha, ha! It is obviously not possible for single individuals to turn out so many words. Mr Trollope, after all, was meant to be holding down a post at the post office. Mr Dickens had a career as an actor. Their publishers rather overdid it, but the public seems happy to be taken in.'

'I must admit, I have often thought that both those gentlemen scribbled rather a lot.'

'There you are then. And while we are on the subject, I will let you into another secret. I myself am known to the world as Preinter. Mr Preinter of Preinter & Preinter's. It was how I introduced myself when you came through the door.'

Herbert nodded.

'I am, in point of fact, the tenth Preinter to occupy this chair. The tenth impression you might say. The original Mr Preinter left the firm decades ago. Whoever sits here and does the work of Mr Preinter, becomes Mr Preinter. This is his pince-nez. When people have dealings with Preinter & Preinter's they like to speak to

Mr Preinter in person and not be fobbed off with some minion who has no proper grasp of the business.' Preinter leant towards Herbert, evidently intending to impart some significant literary gossip. 'At Lawrence & Mayhew's this practice caused a funny situation a few years back. There had been the usual succession of able men working quite happily as Mr Lawrence and Mr Mayhew, until one Mr Lawrence died and the man appointed to replace him was a Humphrey Mayhew. That was fine. He duly became Mr Lawrence. Then it happened a few years later that the job of Mr Mayhew became vacant and the man who came to fill it was a go-ahead fellow called Ronald Lawrence. These two men decided that it made no sense for a Mayhew to work as a Lawrence while a Lawrence was known as a Mayhew—so they swapped desks. It caused quite a stir. No one was surprised when the firm filed for bankruptcy a year later. You can't trifle with the system.'

Herbert shook his head. The subtleties of the commercial world were beyond him.

'But that is all by the by,' Preinter went on. 'Regarding this business, I think you have already discovered that finding yourself suddenly an author of bestselling books has its compensations. Charmian Rivers! Don't tell me you—with an invalid wife—did not allow her to spend the night. Shall we regard it as settled? We will pay you a thousand pounds annually (Herbert nearly jumped out of his seat) to take yourself off to your book-lined study. Never speak of your work except in the broadest terms when it cannot be helped. It might be advisable to purchase a type-writing machine and be heard occasionally to tap at it. Vigorously. Cultivate a mystery around your person. Explain, perhaps to your wife when her nerves are recovered, that all the while she thought you were growing coffee, you were in fact secretly penning a work which has caught the popular imagination. When she thought you were typing letters and invoices, lists and inventories, you were in fact constructing the sentences which have made your photograph famous. No wonder your coffee concern failed; you were too preoccupied elsewhere. Maintain that fiction, and there is no reason why this lucrative arrangement between us should not pertain for years—the amount we pay you to be increased annually in line, of course, with the profitability of titles ascribed to ... Herbert Leadbetter.'

'There are to be more volumes, then?'

'I have staff working on them as we speak. A sequel to *Love's Illusion* to be followed rapidly by ... but you do not need to concern yourself with petty details. Let me instead write you out our first cheque.'

Herbert strolled down Cornhill a happier man than he had been in years. To find himself back in cold, damp England rich and famous! He resolved to purchase a watch and chain, larger and heavier than the one his father had owned that he had been obliged to sell. The sort of watch, indeed, that the successful author of *Love's Illusion* would be expected to possess. How Catherine would have laughed, but even the thought of the poor girl—consigned to her unmarked grave on that lonely hillside on the other side of the world, his stillborn baby in her arms—could not dampen his spirits now.

'If you would be so good?' At the end of the street an eager female thrust a copy of *Love's Illusion* into his hands. 'I have been following you,' she said. 'I said to my friend, Mavis: It can't be! But it is. You are Herbert Leadbetter! I would know your face anywhere.'

'Certainly, my dear,' Herbert smiled affably. He took her pen and squiggled elaborately on the front page. Then he gave her a peck on the cheek. 'I hope you enjoy the sequel,' he said. 'Preinters are issuing it any day now ...'

The girl squealed with delight and gave him a great wet kiss smack bang on his lips.

Herbert Leadbetter would find that book-lined study in some quiet country backwater as soon as possible and establish the ailing Margaret there. He would employ a nurse to take charge of the woman so that occasionally he could journey up to London. Perhaps he would call from time to time on Preinter and enquire how sales of his books were doing. And collect further cheques. Poor Margaret, he thought. He almost felt sorry for her. Authors' wives had a lot to put up with.

FIXING THE GIROUETTE
CHASING CHÂTEAUX 4

'That girl,' Florian said. 'Did you notice?'

'Immediately.'

'It's strange, isn't it? Why would she decide to come and visit just like that, and with her father?'

'Didn't you ask her?'

'I didn't get a chance. They treated me like some sort of chauffeur. It was Philippe at the *Boeuf* who fixed it up. He said they were very keen, and happy to pay.'

'At least we charged them plenty.'

'We did. And they paid up without demur. None of the usual quibbling or haggling. I'll be able to get the weathervane—the *girouette*—fixed at last. And they went off happily enough. The girl seemed to enjoy every moment.'

'I still think you should have asked her.'

'And I still can. I will telephone Denzat at once and tell him to make sure she on no account leaves the premises until I have had a word with her. We will get to the bottom of this.'

'Yes, we must.'

Florian got the car out immediately and drove straight back to the hotel to find Isabel having breakfast on her own. Her father was not down yet and it was probably quite boring for a girl like this stuck in the middle of the French countryside with an elderly parent. Which made the whole business all the more curious. 'Such a pleasure to meet you again, Mademoiselle.'

'Why, um yes! Me too!' Isabel just finishing her croissant had been thinking about Florian and here he was, standing politely at her side. She hastily wiped the crumbs from her lips.

'As it happens I am just driving back to the château. I wonder if you might care to join me. Gratis this time, of course. Come for the ride. I could show you the outhouses. And the stables. We didn't have time yesterday.'

'Oh, I ...' Poor Isabel. She would like nothing more than to return to the Château Remeillant with Florian but she could hardly leave the sleeping Godfrey to his own devices. 'Perhaps this afternoon?'

'*Cet après-midi*? *Bien sûr, Mademoiselle*! I will come back for you at *quinze heures et demi*. 3.30 pm, as you say! On the dot. My mother will give you some more English tea. She did so enjoy your company yesterday.'

'That is very kind of her. I would like nothing better.' Isabel wondered inwardly how on earth she was going to manage things. Godfrey had not at all enjoyed yesterday's expedition. He would hardly want to go back. As it happened she need not have worried.

When Florian returned at half past three, on the dot as promised, Isabel was waiting for him. She rushed headlong out to the car and climbed straight in, begging him to drive away as quickly as possible. Florian assumed she had had a nasty argument with the old man. Poor girl. She needed rescuing.

'*Cherie*,' said his mother, la Contesse Marie Margarita Marianne de Remeillant. 'You came back to us.'

It was a pleasant afternoon. So much better than yesterday when Godfrey had sat so stolidly, making his displeasure and boredom felt. The sun beat down. Isabel wore her new sunglasses and hat and knew she looked her best. Chic even. She was on a second cup of rather strange smoky tea when the Contesse said, 'Tell me, my dear, about the postcard.'

Isabel gaped. She swallowed the tea in her mouth quickly fearing she might choke. 'The postcard?' she said, as if she did not know immediately what the old lady meant.

'It is you in the postcard of our château. We want to know how that came about. We want to know why you came to visit yesterday. We are puzzled. There is more to this than meets the gaze.'

'Eye.'

'That is what I said.'

Isabel sighed. 'The thing is, it isn't me, it's my sister Laura. I don't know how it happened. Any more than you do. We were staying here a year ago and I hurt my ankle and she cycled round all the nearby châteaux. It was a bit of an obsession with her. I can only imagine she arrived here when the postcard photographer, from Bradford, was at work.'

'And where is she now, this Laura. This trespasser?'

'I am afraid I don't know.'

'You don't know where your sister is?' Mother and son glanced at each other.

'No. I have no idea at all.'

'And your father? Does *he* know where your sister is?'

'My father? But he died the year before last. That was really why we came here last year—to try and distract our step-mother. But she wasn't very distractible. Or rather she was entirely distracted. In fact, Eleanor never left the hotel. She sat in the *entresol* when it was raining—which it did a lot of the time—and in the hotel gardens when it was fine. Wearing her black straw hat. And flipping through old magazines. She took no part in hotel life, or in the holiday. I twisted my ankle and Laura rented a bicycle from somewhere and went out each day. Then at the end of the holiday she got the concierge from the hotel ...'

'Philippe Denzat.'

'Him, yes! To drive her to the station. She took a train to Paris. We haven't seen her since.'

'And the elderly gentleman with you? The man who is not your father who you tell us died two years ago?'

'Oh, Godfrey you mean! He's my husband. We met at the Grand Hôtel du Bôeuf last year. That's why we've come back, I think.' She didn't see what business it was of this pair. Laura trespassing and having her photograph taken was hardly any fault or responsibility of hers and yet somehow it was as if her hosts were blaming her for it. Or were they? She scarcely understood what was going on.

Mother and son glanced at each other again, but this time they held the other's eyes. The girl had become garrulous under questioning. It was undeniably suspicious. She was surely covering something up. The Contesse put her teacup back down on the table with a smack. In rapid French, so that the English girl would not be able to catch a word, she instructed her son to go at once to the local *gendarmerie* and fetch the Chief Inspector. 'Be quick,' she said. 'The creature is cunning. She is clearly dangerous. I won't be able to keep her here if she realizes that we know. And I myself might be in danger.'

'Are you sure you will be all right, Maman, left here on your own with her?'

'I have been brave before. I can be brave again.'

Isabel thought Florian had been sent off by his mother to fetch a cake, or some after-dinner chocolates, or perhaps fruit. She sat enjoying the sunshine, enjoying in truth not being with Godfrey. She had slipped her wedding ring into her bag. Why had she done that? Somehow, vaguely, she blamed Laura.

The Contesse Marie Margarita Marianne de Remeillant twisted the Remeillant diamond trembler round her neck and made idle desultory conversation. Isabel answered what questions she understood but now that the handsome Florian was gone, she put little effort into her replies. She began to wonder at what time she ought to be heading back and more to the point, what on earth was she going to say to Godfrey. Perhaps she could pretend that she had left a silk scarf behind when they came yesterday and had asked Florian to be fetched over to bring her here to search for it. Godfrey would immediately ask why she had not just asked Florian to bring it. He couldn't find it, she would explain, so she had offered to come over to have a look for herself. And yes, she had found it. She would produce the scarf she had round her neck to show him.

A big burly *gendarme*, with elaborate braided tassels and piping on his shoulders and matching braid (without the tassels) and piping on his cuffs, wearing also an enormous waxed moustache came striding across the courtyard, closely followed by Florian. He clicked his ankles, bowed low and greeted the old lady with effusive salutations. Isabel he entirely ignored.

'There is a sister who has disappeared.'

'Oh?'

'And a new husband clearly intending he and his wife—this girl here, although she is young enough to be younger than any daughter he might reasonably have had!—is the missing girl's sister. The couple quite obviously got rid of the girl to double this girl's inheritance. The father apparently died not so long ago. There will be a *succession* to share. In any case, the sister has disappeared and neither of the pair claim to know where she is. Or, more to the point, Inspector, they are note remotely concerned to locate her. I feel responsible.'

'You, dear Contesse? How can you of all people possibly feel responsible for the antics of visiting *anglaises*?'

'But I am responsible. The missing girl—who was considerably prettier I might tell you than this dowdy specimen we have here—was apparently photographed outside my château this time last year, when the place was all boarded up, before we came back from Paris. Perhaps she came to Remeillant in her hour of need. To beg for help ...'

'Let me say at once, the whole village is delighted, your most esteemed ladyship, our very dear, our very own Contesse, that circumstances have permitted you and your equally esteemed son to have returned to us. At long last. The place, indeed the whole village, has not felt the same without you, and with the château unlived in ...'

'I am sure.'

'But you can also be sure that we in the Remeillant *gendarmerie* took very good care to protect the place, on your behalf, from trespassers and looters. On a few occasions during the war—the unfortunate times, I should rather say—pictures and other valuable artefacts were undeniably taken. Boys routinely helped themselves to things they could reach with sticks through windows they had prised open. Boys are boys but rest assured, everything identified as having been pilfered in this way was confiscated, severe punishments were meted out and all such articles thoroughly cleaned and returned to the château. We were assiduous Ma'am, in doing our duty.'

'I don't doubt it. I don't doubt it at all. You and your men did your job well, Inspector. But now, I think you had better do your job well again. This creature, innocent-enough looking you might think at first glance, in her silly shapeless English hat and that ridiculous scarf tied at her neck, is clearly dangerous and a threat to all right-minded people. You need to take her in at once for questioning. Then go and interrogate that boring old husband of hers, a most unpleasant customer whom you will find staying for no reason at all that I can discern at the Hôtel du Bôeuf. Philippe Denzat there will assist you in every way, I am sure. Charge the pair of them. If they can't produce the girl, or her body, you know what best to do.'

'It might be as well to try the pair in Paris,' Florian added anxiously. 'Avoid any local scandal.'

'You had better come along with me, Miss,' the Chief of the local police said to Isabel. He had decided that if she came nicely, he might not use his handcuffs. She came very nicely. She assumed, quite reasonably, she was being given a lift back to the Hôtel du Bôeuf.

I HAVE BROUGHT YOU A PEACH

'GOSH!' THE GIRL DROPPED PETER'S ARM AND rushed past Eileen into the room. 'Wouldn't this just make the most wonderful studio!' she enthused, dancing over to the window. 'And what a lovely view! A studio needs a nice view ...'

Eileen, still standing in the doorway, blinked. 'Well, yes,' she agreed, 'that is what it is, I suppose: my studio! Though I usually call it my study ...'

The girl did not appear to hear her. She turned to Peter who was now beside her, looking out of the window also, his arm wrapped protectively around her slender waist. As if she needed protecting from anything, Eileen thought.

The girl laughed. 'Just think, I could do all my painting here. It's simply perfect!'

Eileen blinked again. It's as if I am dead, she thought, and this girl is taking over my own precious room. In the same way that she has already taken over Peter, my son. As if I do not exist. Have never existed. Who does she think gave birth to him, and brought him up? Fed him, clothed him, sent him to school every day for fifteen years. Am I becoming hysterical? she wondered.

'Obviously it needs better light. I could easily enlarge this window, or maybe put in another window. Over there! You could bash a hole in that wall ...'

'I'd rather you didn't,' Eileen said. 'Bash a hole in my wall, that is.' Again no one took any notice so she had to wonder if she had actually spoken out loud. Perhaps she hadn't.

'And in any case, the walls would need to be painted white. Heavens, this wallpaper should be in a museum. Seventies Laura Ashley, by the look of it. You can never have enough white wall space, you know.'

Eileen wanted to say that the wallpaper was, in point of fact, *eighties* vintage. She and Maurice had spent a happy weekend back in 1987, the summer she had been expecting Peter, putting it up. She had measured and cut the strips while Maurice had wielded the thick badger hair brush, getting paste all over himself as well as all over the wall. They had enjoyed themselves and been very proud of their handiwork, although they had never done any more wallpapering.

Eileen decided to leave the young people to it. She wasn't sure now why she had offered to show her son's new girlfriend round the house. Perhaps she hadn't actually offered. It had somehow just happened.

Back downstairs, in the dining-room, she said to Maurice, 'What do you think of this girl? Do you think she will last?'

Maurice behind his newspaper did not hear her. Or affected not to. She began tidying away the breakfast dishes. As she did so, she listened out for movement upstairs. No, the girl would not last. Most of Peter's girls only visited the once. There had been that girl he had known at college who had come about three or four times. But was nowhere to be seen when he graduated and they had taken him out for lunch to celebrate his 2.1 degree. He had been very down at the mouth not to have got the first he was convinced he deserved so it had not felt much like a celebration. The girl had been invited along, and the table booked for four, but for some reason never explained she had not appeared and the waiter eventually cleared away her place and they had not seen or heard anything of her since. Shirley, was it? Cheryl? No, she had been the one after the one who had come next. Whatever was her name?

Eileen unstacked the dishwasher with last night's dinner things and put the plates and pans away. Then she began restacking it with the breakfast things from this morning. This was the trouble with late breakfasts. They didn't let you off making lunch but the meals ran into each other.

The dishwasher worked overtime. As did she! Eileen thought of the translation work waiting for her back upstairs. The deadline wasn't far off. She wondered if she dared suggest to Peter that he and ... what was her name? The girl who was going to take over her pretty room, put a new window in, enlarge the existing one, strip her wallpaper and paint the walls white! What a cheek. Eileen shook her head. In her early sixties, wasn't she too young to be getting Alzheimer's—the heart problem, that was another matter. And one she had not mentioned to Maurice. No point in him worrying. But what was this girl called? They must have been told last night when the couple arrived, but really she couldn't remember.

Suddenly they were there in the kitchen beside her. Peter with his arm round the girl's shoulders. 'Mother,' he said. 'We are going to make the lunch.'

'Oh, no, that's not necessary.'

He laughed. 'No arguments! Mother is very possessive about her kitchen,' he said to the girl. 'But we're not listening, are we? We are not taking no for an answer.'

They laughed. 'We have it all planned,' the girl said. 'We brought all the ingredients with us.'

'That's very kind. Um, very thoughtful. Well, thank you then. I will leave you to it.'

'Can't have you slaving away all weekend!' Peter laughed.

She thought, I don't see why not. I have slaved away every weekend for as long as I can remember.

The girl said, 'I like the cooker. Nice colour for an Aga. It is an Aga, isn't it?'

'Near enough,' Eileen smiled. 'It's actually made by ...'

Maurice arrived. 'Any more coffee in the pot?' he asked jovially.

Before she could move, the girl had grabbed the coffee pot, removed the lid, sniffed into it, curled up her pretty nose and said, 'There is. But better make some fresh.' While Eileen looked on, this slim young thing without a name had filled the kettle, and was spooning coffee from the old battered tin she had had from all those years ago when she was a student herself and still used, with *Kaffee* printed in beautiful old lettering on the side. Jugendstil. She had found it in a flea market in West Berlin during her year abroad studying and had often wondered what this ancient tin had lived through. What it had witnessed. She had wondered too, occasionally over the years, what had happened to Hans Wilhelm who had been with her when she walked round the Berliner Flöhmarkt. Piling her purchases on his bicycle and then, at the end of the academic year arriving at the flat she shared with two other girls, all language students. He took a peach from a brown paper bag and held it out to her. '*Ich habe fur dir einen Pfirsich gebracht,*' he had said, handing it to her. Stay here Eileen, he added. Do not go back to England. *Meine Liebling.* Marry me. We can go to the *Flöhmarkt* every weekend!

Eileen shrugged imperceptibly and left them all to it. To their coffee from her precious jugendstil *Kaffee* tin. I am becoming sour in my old age, she said to herself as she climbed the stairs and went thankfully to her room—that was not yet become a white studio—and shut herself in. She stood for a while simply staring out of the window. She could hear the murmur of voices below, punctuated with laughter. Lots of laughter. Suddenly the merriment erupted into the garden. Her garden. All planned and planted and tended by her through the years. Maurice was talking ten to the dozen, Peter too. The girl hanging on their every word. Looking from one to the other. Not saying much.

Quietly Eileen shut the window. She turned on the computer and found her place in the text:

When the boy returned home that evening he washed and changed and then came back down into her kitchen. He sat himself down at the kitchen table and looked at his mother. Before we eat, Mutti, he said. I have something to tell you.

I thought you might have, she answered, folding her knitting and hiding it—as was her habit—behind the pillow, no, the cushion on the sofa—settee—does it matter? She sat herself down opposite him. Tell me, she said, clasping her hands on the table. Giving the lad her full attention. Tell me all about it, dear.

The boy winced. I think you know, Ma.

I think I might know, his mother replied. *But tell me yourself, all the same.*

All right. He swallowed hard. He coughed. She could see this confession was costing him a lot. She waited.

Then, when he did not speak, she noticed a tiny tear rolling down each cheek, either side of his nose. She recalled that time when he was in the first class at the senior school, the Hauptschule, the High School, and he had come home and sat silently for a long while like this. In that same chair, in this same room. She had been knitting then too. She remembered that eventually the story had come out.

Her son had taken the Headmaster's dog and gone out of the school gate with it and had started for home when the little animal, unused to being off a leash, and without his master, had darted into the road and been run down by a big cart of hay. She had been obliged to pay the Headmaster a substantial sum. The man had not come himself but sent two representatives on his behalf to agree terms. She had tried to explain to these men that her husband, the boy's father, had died the year before in the railway accident up the line but they had not wanted to know. They must have heard about the insurance hand out, though, because the sum they named, to be paid forthwith and in full, was the exact same sum these men had asked for. She had had no choice but to pay. That evening, when the burly representatives of the Headmaster returned for the money and stood at her kitchen table counting it out—every pfennig of it— meanwhile making jovial but unpleasant remarks *about her abilities as a mother, and about her son and his talents as a schoolboy, and then departed, the boy who had sat silently through all this staring at the proceedings as if in disbelief, put his head in his hands. When she spoke to him he had lifted his face towards her and there had been a tear, running down each cheek on either side of his nose.*

She had said, don't worry, son. We'll manage. If it hadn't been this, it would have been something else. They knew we had your poor father's insurance money. They wanted it. That's money for you. If you have it, men like them will come and take it.

But the boy was not thinking about the insurance money. He had sniffed and said, The dog is dead. Bruno. Dear Bruno.

Why did you take him? she had asked the eleven year old.

Because the Headmaster is a mean cruel man.

You shouldn't speak about your Headmaster like that. You must be respectful.

I cannot respect him. I saw him beat the poor animal with his belt. The way he beats me. I know how much it hurts but dear Bruno was tied up. He hit him on the nose. He yelped and cried. I yelp too, but I do not cry ...

She said to her son now, You had better tell me. I should know exactly what has taken place. Exactly what you have got caught up in.

He nodded. I will try and tell you everything before they come for me, Ma. When the police arrive, they will no doubt say all kinds of things you will not like but whatever they tell you, it will not be not the truth. This is the truth ...

Eileen had not heard her own son coming into the room. She jumped when Peter said, 'There is something I want to tell you.'

She swiftly saved her translation work and switched off the computer. Peter was now looking out of the window, gazing down at his father and the girl in the garden below. Eileen looked too. Maurice was certainly in high spirits. No hiding behind a newspaper with that one, she thought.

Peter said, 'I just wanted to tell you this is serious. I am going to ask Nellie to marry me.'

'Nellie!'

'Yes. That's her name.'

'Is that Nelly with a 'y', or with an 'ie'?'

'What? Oh, oh I see what you mean. I think it's a 'y'.'

'You don't sound sure.'

'We are talking about my girlfriend,' Peter laughed too. 'My wife to be. The mother of my children to be, possibly, and the mother of your grandchildren if there are to be any! I couldn't care less how she spells her name.'

'No. No, I don't suppose it ... matters to you. Anyhow, Peter. I am glad you have found someone you like so much.'

Afterwards Eileen couldn't remember what she and Peter had talked about while they stood together in her room watching the garden. Then they had gone downstairs and eaten the 'light lunch' the young couple had prepared. It turned out to be a bag of tomatoes tipped into a bowl, some cheeses on a plate and a huge heavy loaf of bread. She had excavated the fridge and found some butter. All the while, her son and the girl kept repeating the fact that they needed to 'get off prompt'.

Peter and Nelly—or was it Nellie—left as soon as the 'light lunch' was over. The couple had revealed, during the discussion over the meal, that they had been on their way somewhere, some friends getting married that afternoon nearby, so that stopping over had in fact been a way to save themselves the cost of an hotel. Eileen voiced this after the young couple had driven away.

'That's why they came,' she said.

Maurice chuckled and remarked that it was very sensible of them to save themselves the expense and discomfort of an hotel, and then he went off to mend the lawnmower. 'The grass is getting a bit long,' he said. 'You might bring me a coffee,' he added.

Eileen sat for a while in the untidy kitchen wondering how putting cheeses on a plate and chucking tomatoes into a bowl could possibly have involved making so much mess? Ever since the doctor had told her she must immediately set to work lowering her cholesterol (she should never have gone near that plate of cheese!), or he would have to prescribe her strong statins, she had found herself thinking melancholic thoughts about the meaning of life. How fast it zipped by. How little in the end there would be in the end. Eventually, when she heard the lawnmower starting up, she pulled herself together and took down her jugendstil *Kaffee* tin and made a new pot of coffee. *Ich habe fur dich ein Pfirsich gebracht. Meine Liebling!* In over thirty years of marriage, Maurice had never once brought her a peach. Or indeed anything in a brown paper bag.

When Eileen collapsed and died shortly after their visit, Peter and Nellie—definitely with a 'ie'—came back for the funeral. It was very inconvenient for them as they were both busy at work. He had some complicated contracts that needed drafting, she had an exhibition coming up. They agreed with Maurice that it was outrageous of Eileen to have said nothing at all to any of them about her heart condition. The family doctor had not been altogether surprised she had not said anything. 'Patients often keep things to themselves,' he remarked. 'For fear of worrying anyone. Her cholesterol was sky high. She refused all medication—I tried to prescribe statins—she promised to cut out all dairy immediately,' he said.

'Yes, but to have said nothing!' Maurice fumed. 'Nothing at all!'

'She ate a lot of our cheese!' Nellie said. 'How silly of her!'

'She was a lovely lady,' the doctor murmured, signing and handing over the death certificate.

Peter and Nellie stayed in the house the night after the funeral, driving away first thing in the morning. That evening, though, Nellie returned to the house on her own.

'I have come back,' she told Maurice when he opened the front door.

'I have never been so happy to see anyone in my entire life,' the widower mumbled, taking hold of the bag the girl was carrying and ushering her inside.

'I wasn't mistaken then?' Nellie asked softly.

'From the moment I saw you ...' Maurice took her firmly in his arms.

'It's just one of those things, I suppose,' the girl said later as she poured out two glasses of sherry. It wasn't really her sort of drink but it was all she could find when she rummaged in the sideboard. It would do, for now.

'Cheers!' Maurice said, emptying his glass. He was pleased with himself. My goodness, he was pleased with himself! He hadn't been at all sure he still had it in him but there had been no problem at all in that department. The girl may be skinny but she had flesh on her in all the right places. And as for those beautifully pert, raspberry red, surprisingly large nipples ...

Nellie sipped at her glass and wondered what she would tell Peter. But telling Peter could wait. Maurice hadn't been surprised to see her so perhaps his son would not be surprised either when he discovered she had gone. After another top up of sweet sherry, she even, momentarily wondered about Eileen. She had noticed immediately that the few photographs there had been scattered round the house, most of them of Eileen with Peter at various stages of his growing up, were all gone. Perhaps Peter had taken them. He had seemed fond of his mother. She herself could remember nothing about the woman who had lived here, apparently, right up until last week. After they had each had yet another rather large glass of the sherry and had, in fact, very nearly finished off the bottle, she mentioned the painting studio.

'Nellie, my dear,' said Maurice pulling her towards him. 'All *I* want, from now on, is to make *you* happy ...'

'Oh, Maurice, you old darling!' Nellie sighed, nuzzling up to him. She would like to have said that it was surely all any girl could ever want, to have a man like Maurice say she could have anything at all she wanted, but Nellie knew her head was not clear enough to articulate this without appearing a little bit shallow and grasping. And she certainly did not want to do that! Instead, she pushed Maurice gently down into an armchair and threw herself onto his lap.

Wouldn't Eileen, briskly doing her Christmas shop in the local Waitrose the previous December—

first thing in the morning on Christmas Eve—have been astonished if she had somehow foreseen the rapture with which this particular bottle of Bristol Cream, so casually tossed into her trolley, had been consumed! She had naturally expected to outlive Maurice—five years her senior—and had certainly been entitled to think she would survive this festive bottle she had only bought to put in their sideboard in case they had unexpected guests.

By the time Peter got wind of the fact that his girlfriend had moved in with his father, the room that had been his mother's study already had a new window duly bashed into one of the walls, the Laura Ashley floral wallpaper stripped, and the entire room was completely cleared out and painted white.

'It's definitely different,' he said when he saw the transformation.

'Isn't it just!' said Maurice proudly.

Over coffee—from a brand new pottery jar, the rusty dented jugendstil tin having gone in the bin along with the shredded wallpaper; Nellie declaring it obviously unhygienic—Peter told them about his new girlfriend. 'It's early days, of course, but I am sure you will like her. She's called Hetty. With a 'y'. She runs her own business selling upmarket knitting kits. You'll find them in all the big stores. And online. She has her own website, of course. And the funny thing is, she can't even knit!' She's terribly clever...'

The authorities arrived at five o'clock in the morning. They smashed down the door—splitting the wood from top to bottom before levering what was left of it from its hinges. They then swiped the check gingham cloth off her simple kitchen table and sent everything flying. The plates and dishes went crashing against all four walls, breaking into tiny pieces while the Kaffee tin was upended, and her small supply of precious coffee sprinkled irretrievably across the old flag floor. Luckily they did not stop to pick the tin up and look inside, so they had not found the roll of banknotes her son had hidden in there, under the coffee. 'Coffee' that was, in any case, mostly chicory.

They seized the young man from his bed, hitting him viciously about the head with their rifles before dragging him away, bent double, struggling to clutch a blanket as some sort of protection about his naked self. 'Goodbye, Ma!' he called out from under the sweaty armpits of his captors. He had said something else, too muffled for her to catch. Then, after a few more well aimed kicks and swipes at her few possessions, they were gone. Her son with them.

It was, she knew, the last she would ever see of him. Goodbye, my boy, she said out loud. Auf Wiedersehen, mein Liebling Kind. Perhaps cut Kind? Cut Liebling? Leave it in for now. Make my mind up later.

She sat for a few minutes gazing vacantly at the mess all around her and then rose wearily to her feet and set about mechanically clearing up the kitchen, trying to salvage this and that from the wreckage. It would have to be done sometime. Best get on with it.

When she came upon the wodge of banknotes, wedged firmly into the bottom of the dented Kaffee tin, she thought wonderingly that she must have put it there but, try as she might, she could not recollect having ever done so. Perhaps my memory is failing, she thought. Perhaps this is no bad thing.

It did not occur to her either then, or later, that her son had assiduously put aside something each week from his meagre earnings, hiding the money in the tin for her to find should the worst ever happen. A little insurance, he had fondly thought against the arrival of the bullyboys. He had always known they would come for him, in the end.

A few weeks later, when the publishers wrote commiserating with Maurice, and saying Eileen was a sad loss for them also, having been one of their best translators, they said that they hesitated to ask of course, at a time like this, but did he by any chance know if she had in fact finished her latest work for them? She had never missed a deadline before, which is how they had known something untoward was up.

Maurice wrote back promptly—best get it out of the way, Nellie sensibly advised—and thanked them for their condolences and for the kind things they had said about Eileen. He told them how much his late wife had enjoyed working for them over the years, which he supposed was true. He then explained that unfortunately he had not been able to find anything at all on her laptop to suggest she had started, let alone completed, the translation they were enquiring about. She had been suffering, as they had no doubt surmised, from an ongoing heart condition which would most likely explain. He hoped they would be able to find someone else to do the book in the necessary time frame, having learnt from his dear late wife, how crucial deadlines always were in the publishing world. Maurice did not mention that Eileen's computer had been completely wiped. It was a top spec Mac, Nellie had said, dancing up and down in her excitement. She had always wanted one. If they erased everything and then installed programs like Photoshop and Illustrator, it would be perfect—just perfect!—for all her artwork.

JOYCE HAS HER SAY
CHASING CHÂTEAUX 5

'I'M NOT HAPPY. NOT HAPPY AT ALL.'

'I'm sorry to hear that,' Eleanor said. 'But I am sure they will be back soon. If you want to leave a message, I can pass it on.'

'How soon? I hate to tell you—well, I am sure you must already have worked it out for yourself, Godfrey Hutton is not all that he seems.'

'Ah!' Eleanor turned away from the visitor. She wished she would go away. She certainly did not want to listen to anything Godfrey Hutton's peevish sister-in-law had to say. Eleanor began wondering if she could maybe turn on the wireless. Blot out the big woman who had come barging in without a by your leave, and sat herself down uninvited in her living room. She fervently wished she had not opened the door to the apartment. The ring on the buzzer—an unusual event in itself—had been so insistent though, that after ignoring it for some minutes, she had eventually done so. And now this.

'He killed my poor late sister, you know,' Joyce was saying now. 'I am certain of it. Mary told me it would happen sooner or later—and it did.'

Eleanor stared blankly. 'Would you like some tea?' she asked. She was sure there must be some tea and a teapot in the kitchen somewhere if she were to go and have a look. But she stayed sitting.

Joyce returned Eleanor's blank stare, but her own gaze was piercing and furious. She was outraged and found it hard to remain in the armchair. 'Would your late husband have been happy about his elder daughter's marriage?' she asked. 'Are *you* happy about it?'

'Me?'

'Aren't you now responsible? For his two daughters?'

Eleanor wondered how she could possibly be held responsible—why, Laura and Isabel were either side of thirty and entitled, surely, to do as they pleased. Without seeking her permission. Or anyone else's! And how could she possibly be expected to know if Alfred would, or would not, have been 'happy' about Godfrey Hutton? And wasn't it a bit late now to ask these questions. Alfred was dead and Isabel had decided to marry a man she had met on holiday, and why ever not? Hadn't he been kind to her when she had stupidly twisted her ankle riding that great heavy soldier's bicycle? Most attentive he had been sitting with her all day, reading snippets from old newspapers to her and applying some salve the doctor had provided to her swollen feet. Isabel had accepted his proposal and got married with all speed. And very hideous she had looked in that gauzy white wedding gown she had acquired from somewhere. They had presented Eleanor with a photograph of the happy occasion but it was not in any way a pretty picture and she had tucked it away out of sight. Perhaps some food is required, Eleanor thought. 'I am sure I can probably rustle up some biscuits,' she said. 'If you would like a biscuit, that is. I myself don't care for them but I think I saw a packet of *Nice* Laura must have bought ...'

Laura had always been going out and heaving back bags of shopping while she lived here. The *Nice* biscuits must have made their entrance into the Paddington flat in this way, she supposed.

Joyce had no interest in tea and biscuits. It was not what she had come for. All however was explained. Well, not quite 'all' exactly. But she could now see that Isabel's widowed step-mother was little older than Isabel, and clearly not quite right in the head. The mansion flat in Paddington was opulent enough but entirely neglected. Isabel had obviously taken up with Godfrey Hutton to get away. And the girl would get more than she bargained for, and no mistake.

Alfred had spent his career out in India, returning like so many other colonial civil servants on the eve of Independence to rejoin his wife and daughters who were already installed here. Husband and wife had not lived together for decades—Alfred's wife and daughters had not liked the hustle and bustle of India and had come back to London a long time ago. He had been anxious about spending his retirement with a woman and daughters he scarcely knew but he need not have worried. Almost as soon as he arrived, his wife had died. It had been a shock. She had not given him the slightest warning that she was ill. He had buried her, and then married Eleanor, a young woman he had encountered on the boat coming back from Bombay. Neither of the girls had questioned her sudden arrival into their lives. She had no intention of questioning anything they chose to do. And now here was this big woman arriving out of nowhere, smelling of farmyard, and claiming kinship with Mr Hutton, of all people, questioning everything. It was, Eleanor thought, with uncharacteristic but mild indignation, a bit much!

'My poor sister, Mary,' Joyce started up again but just then the telephone rang. This was an unusual occurrence. As unusual as the earlier ring on the doorbell. Eleanor merely stared at the contraption. 'Hadn't you better answer it?' Joyce asked sharply.

'I don't think so,' Eleanor said. 'I don't usually.' There wasn't anyone who might be ringing her whom she would like to hear from.

'If you won't, then I will,' Joyce made towards the telephone but as she picked up the handset the ringing stopped. Whoever had been on the other end of the line had given up waiting, and rung off.

Joyce had come a long way to make this visit, she had had to make complicated arrangements back on the farm to do so, and she was not going to give up quickly. An opportunity might not present itself again. 'Poor Mary,' she began again with only an indistinct idea of what she wanted to say. 'My sister, the late Mrs Godfrey Hutton ...'

Eleanor wished her tedious visitor would go away and she wondered what she could do or say to get rid of her. 'Was there something you wanted?'

'Well yes. And no. Nothing in particular. And yet ... I would like your help.'

'Oh?'

'I am convinced that my sister's death was not natural. She fell down the stairs. So they said. I believe poor Mary was pushed.'

'Who by?' Eleanor asked incredulously. Something like this had happened back in India in those distant days that were not so long ago, but were now very far away.

'Godfrey, of course! Who else? He is a murderer.'

'Gracious!'

'Yes, indeed. I have been thinking long and hard since I heard about Godfrey's remarriage.

To your stepdaughter. Every year he used to drag Mary to a boring hotel in an unfashionable corner of the Loire. Where no one has heard of the local châteaux. And for a good reason. They are not worth visiting. They are not grand places like Blois, Chambord, Azay le Rideaux, Angers, Chaumont ... need I go on? I have been to the local library in Guildford a couple of times and done a little research on the matter, as you can see. The hotel no doubt feels aggrieved that ancestors in those parts had not seen fit to build on a grand scale that would later draw in the tourists, and their money for centuries to come. They must resent the impoverished English who make their way to this quiet corner where there is nothing to do. Mary, though, liked the place. She said it was effortless and Godfrey could be Godfrey without causing too much of a stir. Having met him, I believe you must know what she meant. You evidently found your way to the same hotel. The Hôtel du Grand Bœuf, I believe it is called.'

'Grand Hôtel du Bœuf, I think. It was Laura's choice. Laura's idea.'

'Laura? The one who purchased the *Nice* biscuits?'

'Yes. Isabel's younger sister. She was very keen on the expedition. She wanted to see French châteaux. She was determined to, in fact.'

'Even though there aren't many there? And none worth seeing?'

'I believe she was deceived by an enthusiastic guidebook. In fact, I think the guidebook is here in the flat somewhere. I meant to look for it. She asked me to find it and send it on to her, but I am afraid I haven't had time. And I don't have an address.'

Joyce was not interested in this younger sister Laura. It was Isabel, the second Mrs Hutton who concerned her. 'It is my belief that Godfrey encountered your step-daughter at the Hotel. Fell for her charms and then decided to bump poor Mary off by tripping her up down the steep stairs at their house. And then returning to the Hotel as usual, the following year and this time taking up with the girl and marrying her. This would explain the suddenness. Both of the death of one woman, my sister, Mary, and remarriage to another. Your stepdaughter, Isabel..'

Eleanor gazed at Godfrey's sister-in-law—if that is what Joyce still was now that her sister was dead. She found herself making an unusual effort to think. 'You are, I am sure, completely mistaken in this. We had never been to the Grand Hôtel du Bœuf before. We encountered Godfrey Hutton for the first time on our very first evening there. The girls were certainly not acquainted with him beforehand. In fact, they were far from happy when I took pity on him and invited him to join our table.'

'You took pity on Godfrey?'

'He was on his own.'

'He was a murderer! He deserved to be on his own.'

'You don't know that for certain.'

'Oh, but I do. Who else tripped my poor sister up and sent her crashing to her doom. Mary died after writhing for hours in agony from a broken neck and so many cracked ribs and a punctured lung, and a lot else incurable besides.'

'I am sorry to hear that. But her death had nothing to do with me and the girls. And I am sure Godfrey Hutton, bore though he might be ...'

'Bore he most certainly is.'

'Yes, but I am sure he wouldn't hurt a fly.'

'How can you be sure when, by your own admission, you had only just met him. I observed the man for twenty years. Twenty years in which he made my poor late sister's life miserable.'

'Oh, dear! I hope he is being kind to ...'

'I informed the police of my suspicions.'

'Did you?'

'Oh yes. They interviewed him. They also spoke to the doctor who tended Mary in her final agony at the bottom of the stairwell. They took paint samples from the crime scene. Then they pronounced there had been no crime. Or none that they had detected.'

'I am astonished,' said Eleanor.

'I thought you would be. I thought long and hard about coming to see you and then decided it was my duty as the only one who still remembers Mary and cares about what happened to her, to take the train to London—I came specially, you see—so that you now know the truth about Godfrey Hutton. It's not easy to get away from the farm. My husband had to drive me from Lower Dockenfield—that's near Farnham—to Guildford. And he's all the cows to milk on his own. But if something were to happen to me—a cow knocked me sideways last week. I was lying winded in the corner of our barn and that's when I decided not to put it off any longer ...'

Eleanor could think of nothing at all to say.

'I have had eighteen months to think about it. And when I heard that Godfrey met his third wife at the same hotel he and Mary were in the habit of frequenting, I naturally assumed he had got rid of my sister to take up with this younger woman the following year.'

'Third wife? You mean he had been married to someone else before Mary?' Eleanor in spite of herself was becoming drawn into an interest in Godfrey Hutton's past. Until this afternoon she hadn't given it any thought. None whatsoever.

'Oh, didn't you know? He had been married before Mary, to a nurse he met at the convalescent hospital where he was sent after he'd been wounded in the trenches. I am surprised he did not tell you. He has a son from that marriage who runs the family business. Hutton's Buttons.'

'Buttons?'

'Industrial fastenings. But they call them buttons. You won't find anyone in the Midlands who hasn't heard of Hutton's Buttons. Walter began working there as soon as he left school. He couldn't get away from his father fast enough. The firm is run by Godfrey's older brother although Walter does most of the work now. I understand he and his uncle pay Godfrey a stipend to stay away. It's where Godfrey gets his money from. Hutton's Buttons actually pay him to do nothing. I wish someone would pay me to do nothing!'

'And his first wife?'

'Gwendolyn. She died giving birth to Walter. Mary was very fond of the boy. He was quite attached to her. He doesn't believe the story about her falling downstairs either. But he wasn't happy that I took the matter up with the police.'

Eleanor had woken that morning with the faintest hint of a headache coming on. This was perfectly usual for her, at least since Alfred had died. But now her headache had become full blown, her temples were violently and painfully throbbing. Even so, she could think clearly enough how strange it was that Godfrey had never mentioned his first wife, Gwendolyn, or his son, Walter, or the family business making industrial fastenings in the Midland: Hutton's Buttons.

'I just thought you ought to be told, that's all,' Joyce said. 'I wrote to Walter and said that perhaps he ought to visit you but he said he wanted nothing to do with it. He just hoped his father wouldn't take it into his head to repeat the exercise.'

'Exercise?'

'Although in some ways it would be a good thing. If he takes it into his head to bump off your step-daughter, the police will detect a pattern and have no choice but to take my allegations seriously. Godfrey Hutton had better watch out.'

'Well, yes. But I hope he doesn't ...'

'I had best be getting back. A farm doesn't run itself and my husband is getting on a bit these days. I've said what I came to say. Here—give me a bit of paper. I am going to scribble my address down, so that if you ever want to get hold of me ...'

'Why would I want to ...'

'You never know. Something might happen.'

'Happen?' Eleanor fervently hoped this alarming woman would take herself back down to Lower Dockenfield, near Farnham near Guildford, and her cows, as soon as possible. In fact, this instant! She thought she might be going to be sick. She had married Alfred, the married man she had met on the boat from Bombay, expressly in order to enjoy a quiet life. He had later written to her saying his wife had rapidly failed and might she perhaps consider, now he was free to make the offer, marrying him. He had promised her 'a quiet life'. Those had been dear Alfred's exact words. And now this!

'I will say goodbye then,' the visitor said.

'Oh, yes. Goodbye.'

'You have my details should you wish to contact me.' Joyce pushed the piece of paper across the round wooden table she had used to write on, in Eleanor's direction. She had worked off her indignation that had been mounting over the previous months, ever since she had heard about Godfrey's speedy remarriage.

Eleanor glanced at the large handwriting on the scrap of paper she had given Joyce. 'Thank you,' she said politely. 'I hope you have a comfortable journey home.'

She did not rise from her chair. Joyce hesitated. Was the woman as simple as she seemed? Was she just lazy? Or was she deliberately being rude? She appeared to have none of the normal niceties. She saw no reason to go through with the usual conventions, the standing up, the accompanying a visitor to the door. The utterances of thank you for coming and do come again. That kind of thing.

'I will see myself out then,' said Joyce as tartly as she knew how. And departed.

Poor Eleanor sat where she was for about a minute and then went to the bathroom and was violently sick. After which her head throbbed harder and she was just heading into the bedroom to lie down for the rest of the day when the telephone rang again. Eleanor staggered back into the sitting room and waited for the ringing to stop. She picked up the scrap of paper on which the only words she could easily decipher were Baynes Farm, Lower... She screwed it up and dropped it in the wastepaper bin. The telephone stopped its horrid ringing but then promptly started again. This time she lifted the receiver. It was Laura.

'Eleanor!' the girl gasped. 'I was getting worried. I know you never go out. Why didn't you answer?'

'Laura? Where are you? I wasn't expecting ...'

'No. And you won't be expecting what I have to tell you either!'

'Oh?'

'It's a long story. Listen carefully. I just got off the train in Paris. And read the newspaper.' There was the sound of tokens being inserted. 'This is costing me a fortune. I just hope I've got enough. But I don't want you to worry.'

'Has something happened?'

'It seems Godfrey and Isabel have been arrested and charged with murdering me! It's in all the French newspapers. It's on all the billboards everywhere.'

'But you are still alive?'

'Well, yes. It's obviously some sort of horrible mistake. I am heading to the Hôtel du Grand Boeuf now, as soon as I put the phone down, to sort it all out.'

'Then you don't need me to do anything?'

'No. Not at all. I just wanted you to know there's nothing to worry about.'

'Thank goodness for that.'

'Are you all right, dear Eleanor? You sound a bit ...'

'Oh, yes. I'm fine.'

'Hang on, I need to put another token in the box. I'm running out ...' There was a click and a whirr and the line became fuzzy. 'Can you hear me?'

'Just about.'

'Is everything ok with you? In London.'

'Yes, don't worry about me. But it sounds as if Isabel needs you.'

'It does, doesn't it. I must say, I am tempted to pretend I have no idea what is going on. But I can't do that, can I? They could be hanged for a crime they haven't committed. Although the papers say Isabel is pregnant—*enceinte*—so she wouldn't be hung anyway. And then I could show up and they would release her from prison and Godfrey Hutton would be a thing of the past. But I can't really do that, can I?' Laura laughed.

'No, I don't think you can, dear. Poor Godfrey may be a hotel bore, but he isn't a murderer.'

'So far as we know!' Laura had lost none of her high spirits. 'I had better go. If I catch the next train to Orleans I should be able to be there before the trial starts ...'

'I am sure they will both be very grateful to you for showing up in time to save them!'

'I doubt it. Goodbye Eleanor, I think my last token is about to run out. I had better run for the train. To Orleans. Au revoir, darling!'

'Goodbye, dear Laura. Take care of yourself. Take care of ...' A loud final click and the line went dead.

Eleanor placed the receiver back down on the old telephone. Alfred had promised her a quiet life! She laughed out loud. Then she switched on the wireless and went to lie down in the bedroom where she hugged the turquoise quilted bedcover she had brought with her back from India. There had been murder and mayhem there but somehow she had got away. The police investigation had been thorough and dragged on, but in the end they had proved nothing. Alfred had read all about it in the local newspapers and had assured her, as they strolled up and down the deck as the boat glided through the Suez Canal, that he believed completely in her innocence. 'You poor dear girl,' he had said. 'What a terrible thing to have happened to one so young. And so beautiful.'

AGNES

AGNES IS (ANOTHER ONE) HAPPILY DREAMING. THE
seraphic smile on her shuttered face betrays the
happiness of her dream but reveals nothing of the
violent scenes of carnage and destruction that are
taking place all around Agnes as she sleeps.

First off, she had visited her agent. This
being the celebrated Jennifer Jenson-Smythe.
Expensively dyed hair, trim Italian suits.
Formidable reputation and supercilious smile
that has sent many a writer to the brink of
suicide, for the favour of JJS, or lack of it, can
make or break an author. Just like that (click of
fingers). Poor Agnes no longer enjoys the favour
of JJS—if she ever did.

The first twenty-five minutes of the half hour
is spent listening to the woman, or rather not
listening to her, as she recounts some scene from
her domestic life involving famous composer

husband, spoilt daughter or diabetic cat. For five minutes the matter of Agnes's unsold novel is addressed. We had interest but sales of your earlier books were slim.

They were slim, Agnes says because you have never done anything to help them, even if that is your job. You never once told the lazy publicity people at the last publishers to do anything to promote my books but meanwhile your own self-important assistant cheerily explained to the man from the BBC that my last novel was far too complicated to be abridged on radio, even though I had found a producer who was keen on doing it. And you took offence when I pointed out that this hadn't exactly been in my interest!

That's as maybe, Jennifer smiles. She glances pointedly at the door. She is looking forward to her lunch. She makes a show now of reading her watch. All we can do is keep trying, she says, standing up. Agnes's half hour is up. Agnes has no right to half an hour, only successful authors are allowed half an hour of JJS's valuable time but Agnes has lost sight of this because Agnes was once on her way to becoming a successful author. Three novels well reviewed would have bought her the right to half an hour of her agent's time but Agnes's new novel has been a problem. The publisher agreed to take it. Jennifer had been furious and flexed her agent's mighty muscles and said all kinds of things needed doing to the manuscript before it was ready for publication.

By the time Agnes had finished doing 'all kinds of things', there was a new editor at the publishers who wanted new authors.

The assistant of the departed editor invited Agnes for lunch. A lunch Agnes found herself paying for. Do you want the good news or the bad news first? Emma had asked merrily as the pair sat down opposite each other in the little trattoria in Bloomsbury.

You had better tell me the bad news, Agnes said.

We are going to have to rethink taking your novel.

Oh.

That's not to say we won't take it, it's just that a new editor has been appointed and he will have to decide.

I see. Pause. And the good news?

I'm going to have a baby!

Congratulations.

I'm leaving ...

When the bill came, Agnes had to pay it. Emma made it clear there wasn't a budget at the publishers to pay for lunches with ex-authors.

As soon as she was round the corner Agnes telephoned Jennifer Jenson-Smythe. Can I come and see you, she said. There's now a problem with the book. There's a new editor apparently and new brooms sweep clean ...

Don't worry about it, Jennifer had laughed. I'll get it sorted. She certainly wasn't going to lose any sleep worrying about Agnes and her novel!

But can I come and see you to discuss what to do now, Agnes persisted. She had a train to catch and didn't know when she could afford to come again to London.

Out of the question! Jennifer trilled. I've got an appointment with my chiropodist. Got to get my bunions fixed.

Oh, said Agnes.

A year had gone by. Nothing had happened.

These things take time, Jennifer said. Someone will buy it. Sometime. But she was doubtful. She had sent the manuscript out half a dozen times and then given up. She had never liked Agnes anyway. Far too opinionated for a lowly writer. Not at all well connected. What was in it for Jenson-Smythe? She could not remember now why she had agreed to represent Agnes in the first place. And here was the wretched woman coming to see her again, wasting another half hour of her precious time. A half hour she had no right to.

Agnes looks at JJS appraisingly. Then she produces a hand-grenade from her pocket and rolls it under the agent's desk. It explodes at once, taking letters, manuscripts, publishing agreements, books by more celebrated authors in dozens of different translations, letters about television series, options on film rights, filing cabinets flying through the air revealing their contents, and bottles of gin rain down and smash ...

As Agnes walks away from the scene of mayhem down the trendy cobbled mews, the agent's head flies past her and crashes into the wall, still talking.

Agnes smiles in her sleep. To think that that head with its expensive cut of dyed hair should even now be sitting over a rocket leaf dipped in balsamic vinegar and a glass of chilled sauvignon blanc somewhere in Notting Hill.

HAPPY EVER AFTER
CHASING CHÂTEAUX 6

YOU MAY THINK YOUNG LAURA DESERVES A HAPPY
ending. Maybe you do and maybe you don't. Why
should *she* enjoy ... I hear you thinking. What has
she ever done to deserve ...

In any case, and just as well for Laura, what
you and I think is of no consequence. It went like
this:

Laura put the phone down on Eleanor in
London and ran for the next train to Orleans. She
only just made it. At Orleans she caught a branch
line (*embranchement ferroviaire* as they call the
lesser railway routes in France, where the trains
are often empty and generally arrive late, if at all).
She was then lucky to find a waiting taxi prepared
to take her at once to the Grand Hôtel du Bœuf.
The driver assumed she was another journalist
come to cover the *scandale anglaise*. He was
delighted to discover she was English herself and

asked her quite intelligently if she was writing for the *Times* or the *Daily Telegraph*. Perhaps even the *Express*? Maybe she could get him the autograph of Rupert the *ours*? Laura, good-natured as ever, said she would do her best. He then told her she would be fortunate to get a room at the Grand Hôtel since he knew for a fact the place was full up. Not a room or even a broom cupboard to be had. The hotel was packed out with journalists and photographers who had come from all over France to cover a good story. A very English crime, they were saying. As it happened, though, Laura was in luck. His aunt had a spare room. Perhaps he could arrange ...

'No,' Laura thanked him and told him firmly that she would take her chances at the Grand Hôtel du Bœuf. Philippe Denzat was a friend.

'Ah, Monsieur Denzat!' the taxi-driver almost spat. 'The man is raking it in. He cannot believe his luck having a *vraie scandale* on his premises.'

This was true. Philippe Denzat had received more tips in a week than he had pocketed in the last five years. Meanwhile his employers, the hotel's owners whom no one ever met, were extremely happy. Business was at better than the best pre-war levels. Good times assuredly lay ahead again. They had already started planning an attractive extension at the back of the hotel to accommodate the upsurge in guests that must surely follow such sensational publicity. They cunningly directed the local gendarmerie to dig for a body on the very patch of land behind the hotel where they would need to dig foundations for the planned extension. 'We may as well get the work done for us,' they said.

As it happened, Philippe Denzat's soldier son was back home (with an arm in a sling) and had been put to work martialling the press and the continual stream of onlookers. If a body was discovered, they would be the first to know, he promised everyone who pressed a hundred franc note into his hand sideways. These he duly shared with his father.

And then ... and then ... to everyone's astonishment, surprise, excitement and, yes disappointment (for there were those present who would be quite happy to see Godfrey Hutton hanged) Mademoiselle Laura walked in! Bold as brass. A cheery smile on her face. 'Here I am,' she announced breezily to the foyer at large and to her friend, Philippe, in particular. Of course, the soldier son fell instantly in love with the English girl who had once rented his bicycle..

Oh, you can imagine the buzz, the brouhaha, the consternation. Police headquarters were informed. They called off their men digging for a body round the back of the hotel. The residents of the Château Remeillant were also immediately informed and as a result, Florian and his car arrived shortly afterwards to drive her to the court. His mother sat stolidly in the back seat. Laura laughed the whole way.

'She has resilience,' the old lady thought approvingly. 'de Remeillants have always needed resilience. It was how the family had managed to keep hold of their château and the adjoining lands through all these years. The Revolution, the Vendee, the Germans ...'

The judge laughed his head off (Laura's merriment was clearly infectious). He banged his gavel, dismissed the case and released the culprits, telling them to go home and behave themselves.

Isabel went meekly with her sister.

'Please would you be so kind as to drop us both back at the Grand Bœuf,' Laura said in her impressive, newly acquired French.

'Absolument non!' declared the Contesse Marie Margarita Marianne de Remeillant. 'We will drop you nowhere. You are both coming with us. I want to keep an eye on you girls.'

Now they had the girl in the postcard in their clutches they were keeping her, they said. Half serious, half joking.

There followed a spring wedding: Laura's to Florian. And a spring baby: Isabel's. She called the little boy 'Billy'.

Godfrey Hutton, meanwhile, was left to make his own way back to Blighty. No one gave him a moment's thought, let alone offered him a lift anywhere. He went to Lower Dockenfield, near Guildford, and begged Joyce to take him in. It is what Mary would have wanted, he told her. In truth he couldn't think of anywhere else to go. He had rang the doorbell at the flat in Paddington as that had naturally been his first port of call, his wife owning a part share in the place which you would think would count for something, but no one had answered. Joyce and her husband conferred together and mindful how they were getting on in age themselves and were in need of help about the farm, they gave him a room above the cowshed to sleep in and, amongst other things, put him to work milking the cows every morning at the crack of dawn. One morning, though, he did not get up. Joyce, had heard the agitated cows mooing and when she poked her head into his room, she screamed at her late sister's sometime husband for being ungrateful and lazy but when she went over to shake the bed clothes she discovered he had had no choice in the matter. He had not been able to get up at sunrise to do that morning's milking because he had died some time during the night. An uncanny smile had settled on his frozen lips. He had plenty to smile about, Joyce thought sullenly. Godfrey Hutton had got away with nothing short of murder. Although of course, this had never been proved to anyone's satisfaction, but her own.

When the old lady, the Contesse de Remeillant, eventually passed on, Laura inherited the resplendent Remeillant jewels. Pearls and diamonds beyond her wildest dreams.

The soldier son of Philippe Denzat who had declared undying love for Laura and who had to be continually rebuffed, of course, never married and tirelessly maintained his ardour for the girl who had once hired his clunky old bicycle that had been left in the village by a departing German. His services were to come in handy on numerous occasions, Laura ringing through to the Hotel du Grand Bœuf and begging him to discreetly come to her aid. He was always glad to be of service. There was nothing he wouldn't do for the new young Contesse de Remeillant.

Walter Hutton had arrived one day from Birmingham to escort Isabel and her son, Billy, 'home'. Home turned out to be the works premises of Hutton's Buttons and later when news came that Godfrey had died to avoid doing the morning milking, the couple were able to marry. Becoming the chatelaine of Hutton's Buttons hadn't exactly been Izzie's ambition, but there you go. (Pedants might take issue with a man marrying his father's young widow, mother of his step-brother, but life very often isn't pedantic. And in any case the works premises of Hutton's Buttons was a very happy place until cheap Chinese imports under Margaret Thatcher would put Hutton's out of business. But that was later and needn't concern us here.)

Over time, and despite the devotion of soldier Denzat at the hotel nearby, Laura learnt, alas, that life as the chatelaine of the Château de Remeillant was not all plain sailing. It was not all it was cracked up to be. Life was not entirely a bed of ancient French roses. Florian took to spending long stretches of time away in Paris with, yes, a succession of mistresses, always returning in the autumn for the great hunting parties that took place across the demesne that had been in the Remeillant family for centuries. These bloodthirsty events offended poor Laura's English sensibilities but she was powerless to stop them. The old traditions of the French countryside were not going to be set aside simply because she did not like the sight of dead deer and wild boar piled up on her front lawn with blood streaming from their spewing guts. They hadn't described anything like that in any tourist guidebook, or depicted it on any postcard! Her and Florian's son was as arrogant and adorable and as proud and disdainful as his father. But Laura got used to it all, and to Florian's regular turnover of mistresses who were in no way a threat to her. They knew their place (temporary), as well as hers (permanent). She very happily devoted herself to her painting which she had started in earnest during her months in the south of France. She set up a studio in one of the turret rooms which had plenty of light pouring in where she would wear her late mother-in-law's diamond trembler while mixing her oil paints and occasionally she would pause from her painting to stare out at the view and feel profoundly content with her lot.

What else would you like to know? Marthe, the woman in Montmartre with all the children hanging on to her who had given Isabel and Geoffrey short shrift that time when they came looking for Laura? Laura whom she regarded as a saint having turned up looking for lodgings a few days after poor Marthe's policeman husband had been shot in the line of duty. He had been patrolling the Rue Royale when rival gangs of thieves had opened fire on one another. Marthe's husband and the father of all those small children had been, in official parlance, collateral damage. Laura was appalled. She set to work helping poor Marthe get back on her feet. And she paid rent (somewhat too copiously, but given the circumstances the generous hearted Laura could do no other) and this tided the family over until an official pension could be agreed and then regularly paid. When Laura realized she would have no guests of her own at her wedding to Florian, she had sent for Marthe and all the children, enclosing a cheque to cover the cost of wedding clothes for them all. 'Please spend all of this and come as smart as you can,' she had written. After the wedding the family stayed on for a while in a closed-up wing of the château that Laura had opened up specially and then over the years they would come and stay until eventually the children who had loved the open space of the Remeillant grew up and moved away and Marthe came to live on a more or less permanent basis, rejoicing in Laura's good fortune. And her own. She had been on the verge of putting her head in a gas oven that evening when Laura had mistaken her doorbell for that of a woman on the floor above whom she had been told took in lodgers.

And what of the jobbing photographer Laura had met on that first chance visit to the Remeillant all those years earlier? Not long after that encounter, indeed emboldened by the undoubted success of his postcard series of *Lesser Châteaux of the Loire*, he had set up a rival postcard company on his own, much to the annoyance of his erstwhile employers, Vernon Hicks, of Bradford. But Mr Vernon and Mr Hicks, the proprietors, needn't have worried overmuch because the young upstart had no head for business. He soon got his accounts in a twist, and was ruthlessly investigated by the tax authorities (at Vernon Hicks's instigation, of course) and inevitably declared bankrupt. He was lucky to avoid prison but he ended up sitting every evening, all evening, in the proverbial corner of a public house reliving his glory days when girls had queued up, begging to star in his pictures which had sold in their millions right across the continent. He acquired a reputation for cadging the odd pint in return for his boastful loquacity, little suspecting that most of his fellow drinkers bought him pints out of pity. If only he had known Laura's story and been able to spin the tale of the Château de Remeillant! How many free pints might he have been able to enjoy at the *Dog & Duck* or the *Jolly Fisherman*? But truth to tell, he hadn't given the girl with the funny little upturned nose a moment's thought since she had wobbled away from him on that squeaky old bicycle that afternoon, back down the avenue by which she had unexpectedly appeared.

And Eleanor? She is probably best left to the quiet life she had so earnestly desired although one day, some years after that celebrated court case *en France*, someone who had known her in India managed to track her down to the flat in Paddington. There had been a celebrated court case in India also. The man who had gone to prison for killing her sister, his fiancé, asked her forgiveness and she was able to tell him truthfully that she had long since put everything that had happened out East a long time back out of her mind. He and Eleanor had both been accused but then charges were dropped against her for lack of any evidence. This had not stopped the colonial press whipping up a storm, questioning the girl's innocence, disputing her ignorance of the matter and loudly proclaiming that she and her lover had most definitely bumped the sister off in order that they could marry. When her lover had been sent down, poor Eleanor was forced to escape the unpleasantness by fleeing her lodgings disguised as one of the servants, in a turban and kurta. She had hurried to the docks and taken the next available boat to Southampton. 'I have long regretted my part in it, in that for some reason of your own you transferred your affections from

Beatrice to me. I was very fond of my sister. And I have missed her,' Eleanor told him. 'But, if it hadn't been for you, and my having to leave in a hurry, I would never have taken that particular boat out of Bombay. I would never have met my dear Alfred. Or ended up here,' she waved her hand round the stuffy cluttered living room. 'It's not exactly a château, as you can see, but to me it has been a sanctuary. I suppose, then, that I should actually thank you.' So saying, she showed the man briskly to the door. 'Thank you for coming,' she said as she gave him a light shove and then promptly closed the door behind him. 'Good luck. And goodbye.'

THE DAY YOUNG FONSIE STOLE THE FOX

'YOU TINKER!' HER MOTHER SHRIEKED, LOOMING UP suddenly from heaven knows where as the two of them sat side by side on the wall at the end of the terrace. 'You will empty your pockets. This instant!'

'My pockets!' Fonsie repeated, staring up at the angry woman, blinded by the bright September sunshine behind her head.

'Why do you want to see in Fonsie's pockets?' Aine jumped down from the wall to confront her mother. Fonsie was her best friend. Her only friend really. The only friend who was really a friend. Mother was hardly ever nice to him and even then, she had a sneaky way of being unpleasant. Like the Christmas he had been invited to eat with Aine's family and her mother had suddenly pushed a dish of pudding across the table, saying: 'Help yourself, Fonsie! We all know how partial boys like you are to blancmange.' She had then laughed at him for piling his bowl high with bright pink blancmange. 'You are obviously convinced there is going to be another potato famine!' she said, amid gales of laughter. Her own laughter. Aine had winced (she knew well how Fonsie's grandparents on both sides had suffered terribly during the famine). Aine's father winced too, but said nothing.

Lady Clancade was never nasty like this to Hugo, Clarence or Cyril, the simpering dancing partners she persisted in inviting to the house to play duets with Aine. Or games of cribbage. And to learn to dance the polka and quadrille. These boys had travelled with their mothers from neighbouring big houses, coming some distance over the long straight roads across the bogs because none of those houses were exactly near. All they ever talked about was whipping their ponies and how on some recent occasion they had managed to keep up with the hunt, and been right in there at the kill. Fonsie, though! He and Aine could sit on this wall at the end of the terrace looking down the whole length of the long tree-lined avenue and chatter happily all day. They often did this when her mother was away in Dublin. Or better still, for weeks on end in London.

'I have been keeping my eye on you, Alphonsus Madden. And now I am certain I will have the proof.'

'Proof?' Fonsie scowled. He had no idea what Aine's mother was talking about but he was suddenly frightened.

Aine wondered if maybe her mother was speaking again about puddings. Proof of the ... and all that. Perhaps Cook had told Lady Clancade how they had polished off the whole of an apple pie that morning and she had had to send out urgently for more apples to make another. But so what if they had? Fonsie practically lived with them. Wasn't her father going to pay for him to go to Dublin and get an education? And when he was an educated Fonsie, wouldn't he and she eat apple pie, as much and as often as they liked?

Fonsie's own father had been killed fighting against the Germans in France. His name was carved on the war memorial that had been erected at the crossroads in the village. His eldest brother, who had then run the farm and made sure his widowed mother could pay the rent (to Aine's own father), had gone to Dublin the previous year (to see about the selling of some cattle, he had said) and got himself arrested. Her father stepped in and persuaded the authorities that the fatherless boy (whom he could personally vouch for) had been easily led. They had kept Fonsie's brother in prison 'pending enquiries', for months on end, and then let him go early one morning. Driving him in an army truck to Kingsbridge Station and putting him on a train back here. 'If we ever see you in

Dublin again,' they had said, prodding him in the ribs with a rifle. 'Unless you come back here to take the boat. That might be the best thing for you. They want fellows like you in America. Think about it.'

Eamon thought about it. He had not liked the feel of that cold rifle butt in his ribs and had taken the boat. Her father had given him the fare and accompanied him to the Quay in Dublin to see him on his way. Another of Fonsie's brothers took over the farm work and the paying of the rent. Fonsie, meanwhile, would come up to the big house to share Aine's lessons. He had been slower than her to learn to read but had quickly caught up. Lord Clancade, having no son of his own, was determined 'to do something' for the boy. Lady Clancade was by no means keen. Now she was saying: 'There have been thefts in this house these last weeks—thefts!—and I know the culprit. Your pockets, Fonsie Madden. And sharp about it.'

Aine thought: Thefts! It was the first she had heard about 'thefts'.

Fonsie put his hands into his pockets and brought them out, empty. Aine's mother was not satisfied (Lady Clancade was never satisfied). She bore down on Aine's friend and plunged her hand into the pocket on the right, pulling the lining inside out. Then she turned her attention to the pocket on his left. A little painted wooden fox fell on the stone terrace with a teeny clatter. Its tail snapped off and skittered away.

'Fonsie!' Aine gasped. She was furious. Not at the apparent theft of one of the animals from the Noah's Ark she had owned ever since she was a baby but because her mother was standing there triumphantly witnessing her friend's disgrace. There must be some good explanation, she thought desperately as the pair of them followed her mother indoors. By the time they had arrived in the Lilac Sitting Room (as it said on the silver tag attached to the key), she was able to say: 'Oh Fonsie, why ever didn't you tell Mother that I gave you the fox?'

The boy gawped at her stupidly. He had no guile in him.

Aine had enough guile for both of them. She ran upstairs to her room and brought the old wooden Noah's Ark back down. The animals inside rattled as she ran. 'I am very cross with you, Fonsie. I told you to take *both* foxes. What can be the use of my keeping just one? You know perfectly well animals live in here, two by two ...' She lifted the arched wooden roof with a dove painted on the painted tiles and rummaged around until she found the fox's mate. She put it on the table beside the other. 'I said Fonsie could have the foxes,' she told her mother.

'Did you now!' Lady Clancade's cold blue eyes flashed dangerously. She was hardly going to publicly accuse her daughter of lying. No doubt that would come later.

———

Anne—for she was Anne now—wanted to laugh. What a sight! So many little Fonsies! It was too delightful and too funny.

'My grandchildren,' he said with an equally amused shrug as he ushered the children from the room.

He had been widowed, remarried to a distant cousin and then widowed again. He lived with his youngest son (from his first marriage) and the son's second wife. There were some unmarried daughters and another widowed daughter and plenty of grandchildren about the place. Anne knew this from his letter. He still lived on the farm he had farmed all his life, but in retirement now. She wouldn't find it much changed. It would be a pleasure to see her. (It was this remark that had convinced her to come). The older boys had long since crossed the water. One was doing well in Idaho. And of his other daughters: there was a schoolteacher in Dublin, another in Cork, and yet another, a nurse, in Liverpool. All with families of their own.

'Old,' Fonsie said with a mock grimace. 'I'm old.'

Anne laughed. 'Old!' She said. 'Well yes, of course we are old. It's been nearly seventy years.'

'Sixty-eight,' he said. 'And three months.'

He was right. It was her first time back in sixty-eight years and three months.

'And two days,' she said. 'We left on a bright September day just like today.'

'You did, indeed. You did indeed.'

Why had she come? 1921 was a ridiculously long time ago.

'Always a mistake,' old Fonsie said, reading her thoughts. 'Going back never works.'

'Did you ever hear from your brother again? The one my father ...'

'He made good. He had two sons but they both died in the war. On an American ship sunk by the Japs out east. The loss destroyed him and his wife.'

'I'm sorry to hear that ...'

'My own Eamon, now, he came all the way from Idaho one summer, and I saw in his eyes, though he never said anything, he thought it a mistake. Took him two days after he arrived to work that out. We were a disappointment to him. After twenty years' absence he expected better. He was entitled to shamrocks and leprechauns and all the trimmings. He had his smart American wife with him and some, but not all, of his children. They just stood about staring glumly at the fields. The fields weren't as green as he had made out to them. Nothing was as he had said. They all brightened up when the time came to leave. I only hear from him now at Christmas. A glossy American card. The occasional photo ...'

If only, she thought, if only, if only, if only ...

'It's a joy to see you though, Fonsie,' she said.

'Fonsie and I were the best of friends,' she addressed the child who had returned to the room and was clambering up onto his lap, staring at her all the while as he—or she, Aine was not sure—did so.

'She means Grandda,' Fonsie told the child tousling its hair. 'This lady and I were once good friends. Way way back before you were born. Now, you go and play. Leave me to talk over the old times. Yes, that's right. Shut the door.' When the child had left them, he said: 'And you yourself, Aine? You have children? You did not say.'

'Three daughters. They all have children of their own now. One of them also lives in America. She teaches at a university in New York. My youngest, Antonia, brought me here. She drove all the way ...'

'She dropped you at the gate. I was watching from the window. Why didn't she come in?'

'I told her not to. I wanted to see you on my own,' Anne said, although this was not strictly true. Antonia had not wanted to come in. She had not wanted to drive all the way from London to Holyhead to catch the boat. She said it was mad tripping down memory lane but—this with a big sigh—if it was what her mother truly wanted ... It was. When they got here, Antonia said, 'I'll leave you to it. I will be happy enough pottering about the area. I'll come back at five.'

'I had a son,' Anne added. 'He died.'

'I am sorry to hear that, Aine.'

'I blame the Noah's Ark,' she said, blurting it out before she could stop herself.

Fonsie turned on her the bright beady black eyes she remembered so well. It was strange to see them glittering out from an old man's face.

'If only I had held onto it, I might have ... no, this is stupid talk. Stupid.'

It is what you always did to me, Fonsie, make me do and say foolish things. Things that were in my head. Things my mother could not like. I was never a blurter once I got to London. I learned to smile politely and never give any of my thoughts away. But here I used to chatter without a care in the world. And here she was now, chattering away again. Was it something in the Kilkenny air?

'I have enjoyed my life,' she said. 'I live in France most of the time now. I have a lovely studio. An *atelier*, where I write and paint ...'

'I know. You are famous, Aine.'

'I wouldn't say that. I have the odd exhibition. But you, Fonsie. You have stayed here all this time?'

'All this time. But there's something ...'

'My parents, my father was very fond of you.'

'But not your mother. The Lady Clancade.'

'No. She wasn't ever at all fond of anything. Or anyone. Least of all me.'

'Least of all me, you mean!' Fonsie laughed. 'She called me a tinker.'

'Didn't she just! She wasn't a happy woman. She knew my father had someone else. In Dublin. But there was nothing she could do. She had to keep up appearances at all costs. That's the way it was in those days. Still is, I imagine, with some people.'

Fonsie pondered for a moment. 'Well, now, I never knew that.'

'I myself only found out later. At his funeral. She was there with two children, at the back of the church. One of them about my age. My mother had to pay her off. To avoid a scandal. The woman said she didn't want paying off. But took the money all the same. And asked for more. My mother said she was glad it was out in the open. I had been foolishly fond of my father and it was for the best that I learnt the sordid truth.'

'It explains a lot,' Fonsie said. 'It explains the bitterness in the poor lady.' He shook his head. A lifetime of hating—no, despising—Aine's cold cruel mother fell away from him in an instant. And yet. And yet. How could he feel sorry for the woman? After what she had done to him!

'I ...' Anne hesitated. Then she blurted, 'Can I ask you something, Fonsie. Something that has been on my mind all these years.'

'It's the thing you came back to ask me?'

'In a way.'

'You can ask me anything, Aine. You know that.'

'They burnt Clancade House down because of her, didn't they?'

Alphonsus Madden stared at his English visitor.

She went on: 'Because of the way she treated people. People like you.'

'These things are not spoken of, Aine,' Fonsie said gently. 'They never were spoken of. These things happened, there's no denying ...'

'I'm sorry. I forgot. This is Ireland.'

'But your family had a grand house in London. You were able to live there? Regent's Park, wasn't it? Near the zoo. I looked on a map once and saw you had your own Noah's Ark full of real live animals close by.'

Anne laughed. 'Yes, so I did. I never thought of it liked that. I loved going to the Zoo.' (She hadn't loved it at all. Every time she had been she had found herself unreasonably sad not to have her friend Fonsie with her). 'The house was on night bombed in the war. Luckily no one was at home at the time. I was away doing war work at the Admiralty. Drawing maps.' She did not tell him it was where she had been when her first husband was killed. Hugo, the dancing partner who had often come with his mother across the bogs. They had followed the Clancades to London and resumed the acquaintance. Her mother had been keen on the match and Anne had stupidly thought that somehow being married might keep her mother at bay. She saw no reason to tell Fonsie this. There was a pause, then she said, 'I see the old park here has been turned into a craft centre. I saw a sign to it as we came along the road.'

'One of my daughters once had a job there once. Selling Aran jumpers. And pottery.'

'I might call in on my way home,' Aine laughed. 'And buy a pot.'

'Shall we be walking over there now?' Fonsie asked. 'For old time's sake. We still use the old barn at the side where we keep tractors, and the like. For spare parts.'

'Why not?' Anne said, getting up. Her back ached from the long journey sitting bolt upright in Antonia's car. The car was comfortable enough, in fact it was very plush, but it had been a long drive. Tonight there would be another long drive home.

'Will I be giving you my old arm now?' Fonsie said.

They held each other's arms. Tightly. So much unspoken, she thought. He had been the first boy—the only boy really—who had kissed her. After him there had been men with men's ideas of what they wanted and what they would take. Their kisses were needy and hungry and not altogether welcome.

His family were no doubt amused. They could feel countless pairs of eyes on their backs watching from the windows of the farmhouse as they set out.

'It's Grandpa's posh girlfriend,' one of the children said. Her mother nodded.

'She's a blast from the past, all right.' She could have added what she was thinking. Nothing for us

to worry about. Nothing at all. And there was me
awake last night worrying my poor heart out ...

———

Her mother had stood there with her mouth
open, speechless with anger. Fonsie's theft was
to be expected, the boy was ungrateful, fatherless
and Irish. But Aine's betrayal of her was more
than any woman should ever be expected to
stomach. She narrowed her eyes and directed
her wrath at Fonsie. 'I forbid you ever to enter
this house again. You will never be allowed back
into my daughter's schoolroom. You have taken
advantage of the lessons my husband was kind
enough to allow you to share ...'

'All because of a tiny wooden fox!' Aine said
indignantly. 'A fox I *gave* Fonsie. It isn't fair.'

'Yes, Aine,' Lady Clancade said. 'Because of
the fox. You had no right to give it away. That
Noah's Ark was your father's and his father's
before him. It is the Clancade Ark and you
should treat it, and me, with more respect.' She
turned back to Fonsie. 'If you still have any ideas
of going up to Dublin—at our expense—to get
yourself an education, you can forget them. Here
and now. You can stay stupid and ignorant in the
Kilkenny bogs. Where you belong. You tinker!'

And that had been that. Fonsie had been sent
home. Aine had stood, tears streaming down her
face, watching him make his way down the long
tree-lined drive. When at last he turned in the

distance and was no longer visible, Lady Clancade said: 'I will not have you consorting with that beggar boy ...'

'Fonsie never in his whole life begged for nothing ...'

'Anything!' her mother corrected her.

'It was *Father's* own idea to let him share my lessons and send him to Dublin for an education ...'

'And a very stupid idea it was too. Your father should have more sense. I am ordering the car at once. We are leaving for London immediately. It's time you started at a school.'

Poor Aine had sobbed all the way across the Irish Sea. And a very rough crossing it had been. She had lost her best friend. And she had been right. Never in all the years after had she had another companion like Fonsie.

———

They walked up the tree-lined drive that was still intact—give or take the odd gap where one of the limes had at some point in the past blown down—and then they stood together looking at what remained of the walls.

'I wept and wept,' Anne said. 'Of course we knew from the papers what was happening to big houses all over Ireland. But it was still a shock when the letter came from the agent ...'

'Mulligan.'

'Yes, him.'

'I'm sorry for that,' old Fonsie said. 'Truly I am, though goodness knows we had had enough of the planters and their highhanded ways. To think of taking a young boy from his family and sending him to Dublin in long pants to live in a dormitory and do the arithmetic and trigonometry!' He laughed bitterly.

Anne sighed. 'My father meant well and you would have benefitted from the education. By now you would have been a great writer, a politician, an orator. I don't know. You could have been anything you wanted to be. Ireland would have benefitted ...'

'Not me, though. I would have been sick to death for my home.' He sighed. 'For here. Although here wasn't the same after you left. But I never will know what I could have been. What that other life I might have had would have been.'

They stood for a moment together, contemplating what was left of their long vanished dreams.

'I brought you something,' Aine said at last. She let go of Fonsie's arm and opened the catch on her handbag and produced a twisted silk handkerchief from which she shook two small painted wooden foxes. One of them had lost its tail. She stood them up on her hand and held them out to Fonsie. She expected him to kiss her hand in gratitude, laugh, weep, do something. Anything. But he stayed standing still as stone—

stiller if that were possible. He made no attempt to take the foxes from her.

'I have something for you too,' he said at last to Aine who had become, at her mother's insistence, Anne, half way over the rough Irish Sea all those years ago.

She did not hear him. 'It was all I had time to rescue in the frenzy of our departure.' Aine had not even been allowed to choose what clothes to take. It was her punishment for her foolishness in standing up for Fonsie. A maid—a cousin of Fonsie's, as it happened—had been instructed to pack Aine's best clothes but the clothes the insolent girl had taken from their hangers and folded neatly were not in any way ones either Aine or her mother would have chosen to take with them. The treacherous girl had slyly selected to send only items she herself did not want. They discovered this when another maid unpacked the trunks in London, in the house in Regent's Park, but by then there was no one to admonish. Old Mulligan had given the staff their marching orders. He had paid them all off, as instructed, he said and had no way of contacting them. He thought the girl in question had departed for Dublin to take the boat. Aine's missing clothing was probably well on its way across the ocean to New York. He was very sorry, Mulligan wrote, but there was nothing at all he could do to bring the items back.

The Daimler had been ordered to be ready to start at six. The chauffeur said it would not be safe motoring to Dublin after dark. Best wait till next day. Make an early start. Aine's mother refused to listen. She wanted to be on the first available boat out of Kingstown. Or the unspellable, unpronounceable 'Dun Laoghaire', as it must now be called.

'We are getting out of this godforsaken country,' she shrieked. 'We should have gone long ago. I never wanted to live here in the first place.' She blamed her husband for his sentimental regard for his tenants. Which was all very well since he himself spent most of his time in Dublin while she was left to deal with the resulting insubordination on the Demesne. She blamed Aine, too. Lord Clancade had needed a son and heir. It hadn't mattered too much at the time Aine was born because the couple assumed other children would come along. This had not happened. 'It's time you went to school,' Lady Clancade told her daughter. 'It's nothing short of ridiculous a girl of ten who has only ever had lessons from temporary tutors and governesses.' And alongside that appalling Madden boy. It had been sheer folly, His Lordship thinking he could educate a local child in this way just because the father had fought alongside his own regiment in France.

The shiny black car pulled up at the front door early. The chauffeur set to at once loading on the luggage. If Lady Clancade was determined to leave tonight then the sooner they were away the better, he said. They didn't want to get trapped on the long straight bog roads that had no passing points and where cars that slipped (or were tipped) from the tarmacadam could slip-slide along with their passengers into the moist dark bog, and be lost forever.

'If we go straightaway, word will not have got round that we are leaving. We will be safer than if our departure is trumpeted down in the village,' Aine's mother countered sharply.

'There is that,' the chauffeur conceded. He made a show of looking at his watch. A watch Lord Clancade had given him when he first came to work at the big house.

The moment her mother turned her back for just an instant, Aine slipped away. She ran upstairs to the old schoolroom where she and Fonsie had spent rainy days—Kilkenny being Kilkenny there had been plenty of these—and threw open the cupboard and seized the old painted wooden Noah's Ark that had been returned by a servant to its shelf. She set it down on the schoolroom table and opened the lid, fishing around inside for the foxes Fonsie had wanted so much he had been prepared to steal. This puzzled her. Why, oh why, had he done such a thing and brought her mother's fury down on them both? She would have given them to him if he had asked. She would have given him the whole ark. Aine found one fox, then the other—without its tail—and crammed them into her pocket as she heard her mother's frantic calling from below. When she got to London she would post them back to him as a signal between themselves. In the car, in the voluminous darkness of the back seat, she held the little carved animals tightly, one in each hand.

———

'I always knew you would come back one day,' Fonsie was saying.

'It's taken me long enough. I have thought about here often enough over the years. Life just … got in the way, as they say. And it really did.' She had been married twice, widowed once and divorced once. After that, she had been lucky in having men friends whose company she enjoyed but she had kept them all at a distance. Her painting had never been a hobby. At first she had produced pictures to survive. Later she painted because she loved what she did. Her work was in demand. She could lose herself in it. In France, by the Loire, she could go weeks on end without seeing anyone. She liked it that way, even if it made her daughters fret. They had ideas now and then of housing her in their annexes. Anne felt that she had not lived all her life and done all the things she had done to end her days in someone's converted garage.

'I hope you are happy,' Fonsie said. 'I hope you have always been happy, Aine.'

'No, not always. But I was never again as unhappy as that night we left. Except perhaps when I heard about the house. But yes, on the whole I have been happy,' she told him. 'I thought my daughters were my life but they grew up and had lives of their own. They are always trying to organize me and invite me. They send grandchildren to France to check up on me. I do not understand them. Any of them. My painting has been my life. I had a living to earn. We had no money left after the house here went and the Irish rents were lost, and then father's investments, such as they were, turned out to be unsound. And, of course, the house in Regent's Park was bombed. No insurance there either! But that was all a long time ago. A very long time ago.'

She put the wooden foxes into Fonsie's hand and closed his fingers gently over them.

He said, 'I have something for you too, Aine.' Her daughter would be returning with the car at five. They didn't have much time. They had never had much time.

'Follow me,' he said, as he had often said when he had something to show her. When he had taken her to see a badger's sett he had discovered. Or the remains of a standing stone circle, long since overgrown. A swirling of tadpoles, or a bog eagle's nest. Now he did not lead the way. The pair went arm in arm rather gingerly for fear of tripping on the uneven ground. As they walked towards the old barn he said, 'Go on, Aine. Ask me.'

Anne nodded. 'Was it you who lit the match? I wouldn't have blamed you if you had.'

'I won't lie to you, Aine, and say I tried to stop them. I knew full well what they were about that night.'

'You went with them?' She turned her crystal blue eyes on him—the cold clear eyes she had inherited from her Anglo-Irish gentrified mother. He blenched. No point holding back now.

'The others went in at the front door heaving their petrol cans and clutching boxes of matches. I rushed round to the back. I knew where the key was hidden, you remember. But I kicked in the door in case questions were asked. It splintered easily enough. And then ...' Fonsie paused. 'I could hear them tossing the petrol. I only had seconds. I could already smell smoke as I started upwards but still I ran. I ran faster up those backstairs than I had ever run before, or since ...'

They had reached the old barn. It was tumbled down, but one end was still in use. She felt inordinately weary. Why had she come back after all these years. Why couldn't she have let the matter rest. Her father was dead long ago, bless the kind-hearted old stuffed shirt. Her mother too, her troublemaking in this world a thing of the past. Even the woman her father had loved was long gone. And heaven knows what became of her children who were technically a half brother and sister to herself, but apart from that glimpse of them—weeping theatrically—during the funeral, she had no knowledge of what had become of them.

Fonsie continued: 'I grabbed your Noah's Ark and ran back down with it under my arm, the whole thing clitter-clattering and me unable to see where to put my feet, but any noise I made was drowned out by the roar of the rising flames. I shut my mouth, narrowed my eyes and did not breathe through my nose and I tore straight through the smoke that was now spiralling up the stairs. On and on I went, and out of the broken back door and away I ran, coughing and spluttering into the woods where I hid it. Then I returned and joined old Mulligan's son ...'

'Oh?'

'Yes, your father's land agent's son was the ringleader. It was his idea. I had no choice, they knew of our friendship, you see. They called me the English Lord's lackey as it was. On account of the lessons in your schoolroom and education I had been promised in Dublin, but did not receive. They were shooting 'spies' left, right and centre at the time. I had to prove myself if I wanted to go on living here. Or go on living at all. And me only ten years old! So yes, Aine, I was there with them punching the air in jubilation as the flames leapt into the night sky. The fire brigade did not bother to turn out. It would be no use and it might be dangerous. Why risk their lives for something that was better reduced to ashes.'

'And the ark? My Noah's ark?' Anne could barely speak.

'A few weeks later, I went out after dark and fetched it in here.' The old man was now bending down and pulling back hay from a corner of the barn.

Anne watched as he lifted the old painted ark out from the hay. He brushed away stray pieces that had attached to it, then deposited it carefully into her arms. It was smaller than she remembered. One shake and she knew it was full. The only animals it would be missing were the foxes she had brought back.

'Fonsie!' She gasped, hardly making a sound. If her arms had not been holding the ark she would have clasped him to her. Never to let go. The old man grinned.

'A fair exchange,' he said. 'I get the foxes I wanted so badly, you get your ark back.'

They heard a car in the distance tooting. She glanced at the diamond watch that had been her mother's. Astonishingly, after all these years, it kept good time. It was already five o'clock. Antonia would be sitting impatiently in the car outside the farmhouse door, with the radio blaring.

'Has no one ever touched it since?'

'No,' he said. 'It was yours, Aine. It has been waiting for you here in the barn all this time.

Whenever life got hard, and it did at times like when my first wife died and I had the orphaned little ones to look after, and the farm nearly repossessed, I would come out here to grease my tractors and sit with it. I knew that you would want me to find the strength to carry on and somehow, just knowing that gave me the will to do so.'

'Oh, Fonsie.'

They started to walk slowly back to the car.

'We'll meet again in heaven,' he said. 'That's for sure.'

'It's been heaven this afternoon,' Anne replied. 'Who knows what life might have been ... If ...'

'Don't think like that, Áine. It's not right.' He held her hand. 'It's been a great life. I've always had you to love. That's been the best of it.'

She blushed. Eighty-four and blushing, who would have believed it! 'I loved you too, Fonsie. Always have, always will.'

'You and I were animals in an ark of our own making. It had no painted ladder or lid.'

She nodded. 'We were that,' she said. 'No way out, no way in.'

They were silent for a while.

'Thanks for keeping my ark safe, Fonsie. Take good care of the foxes now.'

'I will, I will,' he chuckled. 'After all, one of them cost me dear.' He held up the fox that was missing its tail. When the time came, he thought, he would ask his family to bury it with him.

'Why did you take him, Fonsie? It's the one thing I never understood.'

'Did you not, Aine? Did you really not know?'

She shook her head.

'I often took an animal out of the ark when you weren't looking to put under my pillow at night. Next time I came I returned it to its mate. And took another. It was borrowing, Aine, not theft, whatever your mother said. I liked to keep a little of you by me, if you like. Was it so terrible?'

'No, Fonsie, you old dear. It wasn't terrible at all.'

'I told the priest at Confession once. He said I had committed the sins of envy and avarice and made me do a hundred Hail Marys, or some such. The old fool. I never envied you anything, Aine, stuck in that cold Big House, on your own.'

'Oh, Fonsie, I would gladly have given you the whole ark to take home if I had known. I should have known. But we were children. I thought one day, when we grew up ... But it was an impossible dream.'

'It was. But when all's said and done, impossible dreams are better than no dreams at all.'

They held hands briefly. They had reached Anne's daughter's car.

———

'What's that, then?' Antonia asked sharply as she manoeuvred impatiently back down the rough farm track. Heaven knew what damage the great clods were doing to her undercarriage and tyres, and what Rupert would say when he saw!

What does it look like? Anne thought, clasping her childhood toy tightly to her.

'An old Noah's ark!' Antonia exclaimed after a quick glance sideways. 'I always fancied one of those. They go for a fortune at auction these days.' Another quick sideways glance. 'But only in tiptop condition.'

'Do keep your eyes on the road, dear.'

Antonia concentrated on the road while inwardly resolving that when the time came she would be the one to get her hands on the ark (her sisters having played no part in this expedition) even if it was a bit battered and had probably lost half its contents. After a few miles she spoke again, by way of conversation: 'I called in at the Clancade Craft Centre. It was what you would expect. Tat for American tourists. Appalling pottery and fake Aran sweaters. I had a disgusting cup of tea. A nice slice of plum cake, though. The Irish seem to be able to do cake.'

Anne was not listening. Just get me and my ark to the unpronounceable, unspellable Dun Laoghaire, she thought wearily. Never mind your undercarriage and tyres. Never mind the wrath of your Rupert. Get me out of this godforsaken country. Even if they can do cake! Quick as you can. After a while, she relaxed and reached over into the back of the car to place the shabby little painted ark gently on the seat. I will put it in pride of place on the mantelpiece in France, she thought. She gazed out of the window contentedly. They would be through the long straight roads across the bog before the sun set. That was the main thing.

YOU CAN TAKE THAT!

THE OTHER DAY I CAME ACROSS A CRUMPLED silver thimble that my grandmother once gave me. It is worn so thin that if you hold it up, light seeps through the tiny perforations like memory in a sieve. It is too delicate to smooth out the dents, and part of the rim is missing. The silver is black but I can make out a tiny hallmark with an anchor.

I have a vague recollection of sitting in my grandmother's living room and noticing it on a shelf. I picked it up and tried it on. She said: 'You can take that!' so I said 'Thank you' and put it in my pocket.

Twenty-five years on, when she has been dead a decade, I am surprised to come across it in a drawer. I pick it up and find it a perfect fit though the dents, the tarnished thinness, and the little anchor make me cry.

A Few Notes & Acknowledgements

My first mention is Eleanor Flegg of the *Irish Independent*. If it hadn't been for you telling me that a couple of Vivien Greene's dolls' houses that I had written about for the (UK) *Independent* in 1998 were up for sale again, at Fonsie Mealy's auction house in Castlecomer, Co. Kilkenny, July 2019 and as a consequence having an old wooden Noah's Ark knocked down to me as I tried to work out (in temperatures exceeding 40 degrees) how to bid online ... This disaster then turned into a good excuse to personally fetch said ark, visit Ireland, and meet you. *The Day Young Fonsie stole the Fox* came into my head in its entirety while you were interviewing me about my wallpaper designs. I got so carried away, the contents of the ark somehow flew all over the recording studio and we retrieved them as best we could but left me desperately worried that I might have mislaid a fox. Or two. I then sat up all night in my hotel room in Dublin nursing the world's worst migraine, wondering how I was going to get the precious ark on the plane and writing this story. So, thank you.

The Sequence of Things was written in the first instance for BBC Radio 4 as part of my 5 part series "Snap", April 2006, produced by Pam Fraser-Solomon with this episode acted by Claire Skinner. The episode enacted by Leslie Grantham ("Dirty Den" of *EastEnders*) about a deliciously lewd seaside photographer was famously pulled at the last minute by *Woman's Hour* and the scandal written up, as scandals tend to be, in the *Sunday Times* which gave me no end of grief as I had inadvertently supplied the journalist with the information. This though was a shame as Grantham's performance was stupendous and should have been broadcast and I will publish that story from the series another time.

The Right Face was originally published in *Prospect* magazine, November 2000 and was based on something I witnessed in Ceylon/Sri Lanka. *The Wood Engraver* is loosely—very loosely—based on my friendship with the remarkable wood engraver (some would say *the* wood engraver) Joan Hassall (who did indeed have an Albion printing press, dated 1832 with "a brass label and still going strong" and which is now miraculously in my workshop after I discovered it being advertised on Instagram a couple of years ago). She was in her eighties when I met her and almost blind, and very kind and encouraging to my younger tentative student self.

Regarding the title story, I hope it is obvious I have wantonly mangled memory and actuality. Almost the only truth here is that the Musée d'Orsay in Paris does possess Édouard Manet's *Le Citron* but when I last visited it had been removed from display. No doubt because they are expecting to be mobbed by visitors after my story is published and have sensibly stored it away for safety reasons.

Everything in *Chasing Châteaux* is made up except for the fact that I cycle round the countryside near Sancerre château spotting. It has become a bit of a hobby, some might say obsession, and I always think of Laura and Isabel when I hit a pothole and nearly come off my bike.

Finally I must, of course, thank James and Marian Womack of the Calque Press, Cambridge, late of Nevsky, Madrid for all their belief and encouragement. Enthusiasm. Enlightenment. And editing. I am so proud to be one of the earliest books published by this new venture that will I am sure, with these two distinguished writers at the helm, become the Leonard and Virginia Woolff's Hogarth Press of the future. First editions of *The Lemon Painters* will no doubt be highly sought after in antiquarian bookshop catalogues, especially uncut, unopened, undamaged (and unread) copies. I must also thank dear John and Berry Goss who are still waiting patiently for my book on Lora, Ireland and Ceylon that seems to be taking forever but is still very much in the Cory pipeline. Thank you for your patience and many kindnesses over the years.

Since all good books must be dedicated to someone near and dear, let my husband, "PP", and little Bessie, our highly opinionated fox terrier, whose shrill barks ring out across Sancerre and its surrounding vineyards share the honours as they have so nobly shared my French adventure—and occasional hair-raising encounters with wild boar, not to mention irate *proprietaires*, while château chasing—these last years. I exaggerate. The encounter with the *proprietaire* only happened once and we ended up invited into the dank château cellars for a *dégustation* using grubby but ancient wine glasses with the family crest engraved on them. A crest, I was amused to see, that included a lemon. Or something very like a lemon.

This edition of *The Lemon Painters*
was published on 2 December 2020,
anniversary of the birth, in 1859,
of the pointillist painter Georges Seurat

Lightning Source UK Ltd.
Milton Keynes UK
UKHW012325161220
375296UK00002B/97